THE AMMONITE LANGUAGE OF THE IRON AGE

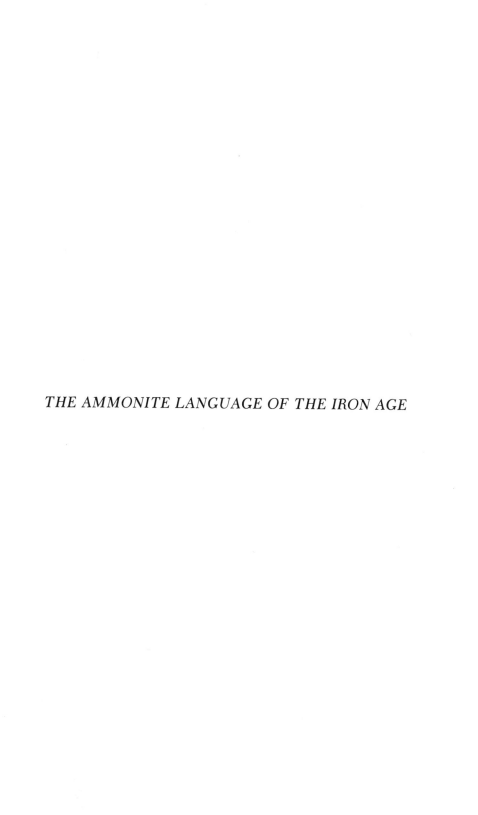

HARVARD SEMITIC MUSEUM

HARVARD SEMITIC MONOGRAPHS

Frank Moore Cross, Jr.,
Editor

Number 27

THE AMMONITE LANGUAGE OF THE IRON AGE

by
Kent P. Jackson

Kent P. Jackson

THE AMMONITE LANGUAGE OF THE IRON AGE

Scholars Press
Chico, California

THE AMMONITE LANGUAGE OF THE IRON AGE

Kent P. Jackson

Library of Congress Cataloging in Publication Data

Jackson, Kent P.
The Ammonite language of the Iron Age.

(Harvard Semitic monographs ; no. 27)
Revision of thesis (Ph.D.)—University of Michigan, 1980.
Bibliography: p.
1. Ammonite language. I. Title. II. Series.
PJ4143.J3 1983 492.4'7 82-16813
ISBN 0-89130-592-0

Printed in the United States of America

For Nancy, Sarah,
Rebecca, and Jennifer

KENT P. JACKSON is Assistant Professor of Ancient Scripture at Brigham Young University. He has been on the faculty at BYU since 1980.

He holds a B.A. from Brigham Young University and an M.A. and a Ph.D. in Near Eastern Studies from the University of Michigan.

PREFACE

This study is a revision of my doctoral dissertation presented in the spring of 1980 in the Department of Near Eastern Studies at the University of Michigan. In its present form it differs substantially from the original, with the inclusion of two inscriptions and several seals which were not available to me when the dissertation was written.

Special thanks are due to Professor David Noel Freedman for his assistance and encouragement as I undertook this study. His generous contribution of time and effort in my behalf was a tremendous help, as were his valuable suggestions for this work. Similarly I am indebted to Professor Frank Moore Cross, whose expertise and instinct for excellence have made this undertaking better than it was when he first saw it, and whose contributions to our knowledge of the Ammonite language are well known. Professor Cross's influence is apparent throughout this endeavor. Acknowledgement is also in order for Dr. Michael Patrick O'Connor, who read all of this treatise as it was being written and who contributed suggestions of much value as well as much-needed encouragement.

For his invaluable contribution—not only to this study—I would like to acknowledge my gratitude to Professor Charles R. Krahmalkov. It is from him that I learned the necessity of a careful and systematic approach to ancient documents. The methodology employed in this monograph—insofar as it has succeeded—must be attributed at least in part to him. Moreover, it was he who introduced me to Northwest Semitic inscriptions originally and who stimulated my enthusiasm for this field under his careful tutelage.

Finally, the contributions of my wife and three daughters, to whom this book is dedicated, are immeasurable.

Provo, Utah K.P.J.
June 1982

TABLE OF CONTENTS

CHAPTER ONE
INTRODUCTION TO THE STUDY

The Texts

The corpus of readable texts in the ancient Ammonite language consists of three inscriptions from ʿAmmān: the Amman Citadel inscription (AC), the Tell Siran inscription (TS; Tell Sīrān is 9 km northwest of the center of ʿAmmān), and the Amman Theater inscription (AT); four inscriptions from Tell Ḥisbān (H 1, 2, 3, and 6; cf. the introduction to chap. 5); an inscription discovered at Nimrud in Iraq (NO); and over sixty seals from various locations in the area of the ancient kingdom of Ammon (AS 1–61). Many of the seals have been known for decades (cf. bibliographical data in Herr 1978: 59–74); the majority of the larger texts are of more recent discovery. The Citadel and Theater inscriptions were discovered in 1961 and were first published in 1968 (Horn 1967–68: 81–83; Dajani 1967–68: 65–67); the Tell Siran inscription was published in 1973 (Thompson and Zayadine 1973a: 5–11); and the Heshbon ostraca were published in 1969 (Cross 1969b: 223–29), 1973 (Cross 1973b: 126–31), 1975 (Cross 1975: 1–20), 1976 (Cross 1976: 145–48), and 1983 (Cross 1983). The Nimrud ostracon was first published in 1957 but was considered to be Aramaic. In 1980 it was correctly identified as Ammonite (Naveh 1980: 163–71).

Since these original publications there has been only a minimum of secondary literature dealing with most of the texts—undoubtedly because of the recent dates of their first appearances. The notable exception is the Citadel inscription, which almost immediately set off a steady stream of articles devoted to its study (for references, cf. Introduction in chap. 2).

With the publication of his "Epigraphic Notes on the Ammān Citadel Inscription" (1969a: 13–19), F. M. Cross began a systematic analysis of the scripts used in Ammonite texts. This analysis has found its fullest statement in his treatment of H 1

(1975: 10–17) and in the work of his student L. G. Herr, whose Ph.D. dissertation included a paleographic study of the Ammonite seals (1978: 55–78 and figs. 34–45). Stated very briefly, the history of Ammonite scripts can be traced as follows. The earliest Ammonite text, the Citadel inscription, was written in the typical Aramaic lapidary script of the mid-9th century. It contrasted in that regard with the contemporary Mešaʻ inscription, which was written in an indigenous south Palestinian script used also for contemporary Hebrew epigraphs. Near the middle of the 8th century, Ammonite developed from the Aramaic its own national script type (Cross 1973a: 13), which it used in both cursive (e.g., H 1) and semiformal (e.g., TS) forms until the Persian period, when the Aramaic script of the Persian imperial bureaucracy replaced it.

Most of our Ammonite texts fall within the period in which the Ammonite script was in use, i.e., H 6 (7th century), TS (ca. 600), H 1 (ca. 600), AT (ca. 580), H 2 (ca. 575), and about sixty seals. AC, as noted above, is in the parent Aramaic script of the earlier period, while H 4 (ca. 525) and H 5 (ca. 500) are written in the later Aramaic script which supplanted the national script of Ammon (as also that of Judah) after the tremendous political upheavals of the early and mid-6th century and the probable disruption—or destruction—of the Ammonite scribal school. With the available inscriptional evidence, it is now possible to distinguish the Ammonite script from all others and to trace internal developments which occurred during the period of its use. It is therefore possible, on the basis of the script, to identify an inscription as Ammonite with some accuracy (cf. Naveh 1971: 27–32). Note, however, the cautionary remarks concerning AS 49 in chap. 7 and the Deir ʻAllā text, below. Nonetheless, true identification of the language of an inscription can only follow systematic examination of the linguistic data which it contains.

The Purpose of the Study

Since none of the larger texts were available to scholars before 1968, the study of the Ammonite language is still in its infancy. Secondary treatments in response to the *editiones principes* are few, and no systematic analysis has been made of the corpus as a whole. The paleographic discussions presented by Cross enable us to describe a distinctive Ammonite *script type* and its history, but thus far no synthesizing study has been made available which enables us to describe the Ammonite language itself. That is the purpose of the following investigation.

In this study I will examine all the known Ammonite texts in order to isolate the linguistic features which make up the language and show it either to differ from or coincide with the other languages of the same time period elsewhere in the eastern Mediterranean region. My goal is to identify paradigms for Ammonite which will show in systematic fashion the characteristics of the language and which will enable us to determine its relationship to the neighboring languages: the various Phoenician dialects, Israelite, Judahite, and Moabite.

Methodology

Each chapter presents one inscription or, in the case of chaps. 5 and 7, a collection of inscriptions. In each chapter, the method of discussing the text(s) is the same. Following introductory remarks, a transcription of the text and a translation will be given. Thereafter I will present notes to the translation and other comments depending on the specific requirements of the text involved.

I have dealt more extensively with the Citadel inscription than with the others because of the difficulty of the text. It has been necessary to treat it fully in order to justify the translation upon which the discussions of morphology and orthography are based. Each chapter contains a complete lexicon of the words found in the inscriptions, followed by morphological charts which isolate the different varieties of words and show their attested inflections or conjugations. It is necessary to analyze each inscription individually in this manner in order to determine whether its language is the same as that of the other texts examined. Next I will discuss matters of phonological and orthographic importance. Orthographic analysis is a key component of this study, as will be seen below. I will use it not only in an attempt to describe the rules of spelling employed by Ammonite scribes—which is a valid study in itself—but also to identify phonological features which will aid in distinguishing Ammonite from the other languages of ancient Canaan. Wherever relevant, the system of word division will then be discussed. Finally, I will present a discussion concerning the linguistic affiliation of each text, in which I will analyze the data presented in the chapter and ascertain whether the language of the text can be classified with respect to other languages from the area and if so to what extent. Chapter 8 will be an analysis of all the data gleaned throughout the study, in which will be found a complete lexicon of all the attested Ammonite words as well as morphological charts of all the known elements of the Ammonite language. The bibliography lists all of the works cited in this study.

Other Texts from Transjordan

We cannot determine the precise boundaries of the Iron Age Ammonite kingdom. We do know, however, that it was a tiny state, centered around the capital of Rabbath-Ammon (Landes 1961: 68–70). It was small in comparison to its sister state Moab to the south, the extent of which is illustrated in Meša''s description of his conquests and construction projects (*KAI* 181). The linguistic history of Transjordan is complex, especially in the period from which the Ammonite texts come. The Iron Age was a time of great diversity, with elements of Aramaic, Canaanite, and Arabic being present in the spheres of language and culture. The inscriptional remains show evidence of all three language groups. In addition to Ammonite, we can outline the main attested languages as follows.

Moabite

This language is attested in two inscriptions. The 9th-century Meša' inscription (*KAI* 181), discovered at Dhiban, is the primary text in Moabite. It is the largest Iron Age text found in Palestine (34 lines), and it contains a wealth of historical and linguistic data. The Kerak inscription (Freedman 1964: 50–51; Gibson 1971: 83–84) is a fragment containing parts of four lines. In addition to these texts, a small number of seals from the 8th to the 6th centuries are assigned to Moabite (Avigad 1970: 289–92; Herr 1978: 153–59 and figs. 75–77).

Edomite

This language is scarcely attested. Herr assigns eight 8th/7th-century seals to Edomite (1978: 161–69 and figs. 78–80). Eight small inscriptions, dating to the 3rd century, were discovered at Khirbet el-Kom in the early 1970s. Though these contain elements of Aramaic, they are classified as Canaanite by L. T. Geraty, who treated them extensively in his Ph.D. dissertation from Harvard University (1972). They are primarily commercial, and some are Canaanite/Greek bilinguals. In addition to these, Cross (1969c: 23) and Naveh (1971: 32) classify the 5th-century Lachish Incense Altar inscription as Edomite. Whether it is Edomite is not certain, but it clearly is Canaanite rather than Aramaic. It is difficult to tell to what extent an "Edomite" language of the Canaanite family was spoken in the earlier periods.

Arabic

The earliest Arabic texts discovered so far in Transjordan date to a period much later than that of the Ammonite corpus. Yet Arabic elements in a few of the Ammonite names argue for a linguistic diversity in ancient Ammon that did not exclude Arabian influence.

Aramaic

The presence of the Aramaic language in Transjordan during the 1st millennium is not surprising, given the strength of Aramean culture, its literary tradition, and the powerful Iron II period Aramean kingdoms. As early as the 7th century, and possibly even earlier (Naveh 1971: 27), Aramaic was a *lingua franca* in much of the Near East, a circumstance that lasted until the conquest of Alexander the Great and to some degree even later than that. It was especially prominent in the Persian period, when it was used as the official language of the Achemenid empire and its vast administrative structure. Five small ostraca dating from that period were discovered at the Edomite site of Elath (Ezion-Geber). Though they are fragmentary and the writing is faint, they have been identified as Aramaic (Glueck 1940; 1941; Albright 1941; Torrey 1941).

An interesting statue was found in ʻAmmān in 1949 (Barnett 1951) which has on its pedestal a short inscription: *]šw yrḥʻzr[/]kr br šnb[*. Zayadine (1974: 135–36) dates the text to the late 8th century on the basis of the names preserved in it, while Albright's 7th-century date (1953: 135–36) is based on the paleography. The script is Aramaic. The word *br* is Aramaic rather than Ammonite, but as Zayadine has pointed out (1974: 135–36), it is probable that the individuals named are Ammonite royalty. Cf. the use of *br* in the Kilamuwa inscription, *KAI* 24. Zayadine has equated *šnb* of line 2 with the Ammonite king named Sanipu in the annals of Tiglath-pileser III (*ANET*: 282). The statue itself probably represents a king. It resembles objects from north Syria, and particularly from Zinjirli (cf. *ANEP*: figs. 62, 455, 530; von Luschan 1911: pls. 58, 66, and fig. 265). Both the statue and its inscription can be explained on the basis of Aramean cultural influence, which may have been quite strong during the 8th century. It is a period from which we have no inscriptions and relatively few seals in the local Ammonite language.

Deir ʻAllā

Early in 1967, at the site of Deir ʻAllā on the east side of the Jordan Valley, fragments of a large inscription were discovered (Franken 1967: 480–81). The text, written in ink on plaster, was published in 1976 (Hoftijzer and van der Kooij 1976). It dates, according to van der Kooij, to ca. 700 B.C. ± 25 years (Hoftijzer and van der Kooij 1976: 96) and, according to Cross, to the early 7th century (1975: 12). Excitement concerning the inscription originally centered around the main character of the text, Balaam, son of Beor, known elsewhere only in the old poetry of Numbers 23–24 and the surrounding narrative material (Hoftijzer 1976: 11–17). Currently, however, the language in which the inscription was written has become the focus of attention.

In the *editio princeps*, J. Hoftijzer characterized the language of the texts as "an Aramaic language hitherto unknown" (Hoftijzer and van der Kooij 1976: 300). He cautioned, however, that the language of the texts need be classifed as "Aramaic" in contradistinction to "Canaanite" only if one insists on a strict dichotomy between the two languages (or language families) in this period (implying that such a distinction is not necessarily called for). This caution was prompted by the existence of several items in the texts which are otherwise rare or unattested in Aramaic and more common in Canaanite, i.e., the verbs *p'l* (rather than *'bd*) and *r'y* (alongside *ḥzy*), the *Nip'al* stem, and the converted imperfect with *waw*-consecutive. Most of the scholars who have published studies of the text have classified its language as some kind of Aramaic dialect. Thus Hoftijzer refers to "an Aramaic language hitherto unknown" (Hoftijzer and van der Kooij 1976: 300) and Fitzmyer to "a form of Old Aramaic," with "a few surprises"—observing the imperfects with *waw*-consecutive and the *Nip'al* forms but pointing out the existence of the *waw*-consecutive in the Zakir inscription (*KAI* 202.A.11bis) (Fitzmyer 1978: 94). P. K. McCarter also retains the term Aramaic for the inscription but speaks of it as a literary or archaistic dialect influenced by "Canaanite literary tradition." Underlying the dialect of the text, according to McCarter, is the spoken language of Deir 'Allā, which was likely "an Aramaic dialect of unexceptional character" (McCarter 1980: 50–51). Caquot and Lemaire (1977: 208) also view the language as a form of Old Aramaic, heavily influenced by Canaanite literary style, while S. A. Kaufman maintains that the dialect of the text is the local tongue of the Deir 'Allā region, and that "it is hardly incorrect to term it an Aramaic dialect, for it shares far more of its grammatical features and distinctive vocabulary with other Aramaic dialects than it does with any other Semitic dialect group. . . . And, surrounded on three sides by Canaanite speakers, it is hardly surprising that this dialect lies on the Canaanite side of many isoglosses (a few, perhaps, the result of borrowing; most, no doubt, the result of shared inheritance)" (Kaufman 1980: 73).

In a recent study of the Deir 'Allā material, Jo Ann Carlton has reexamined the information from the text in light of improved readings of the fragments. In her 1980 Harvard dissertation she offers convincing evidence for readings that differ in key areas from those of Hoftijzer and van der Kooij. In those improved readings most of the seemingly Aramaic characteristics of the text disappear, including *'aleps* that heretofore have been considered emphatic endings. Carlton concludes that the Deir 'Allā texts are written in a Canaanite dialect, not Aramaic. Her evidence is quite compelling. Cross concurs.

The Deir ʿAllā material is deserving of the foregoing introduction because of its geographical proximity to the ancient kingdom of Ammon. Moreover, the texts share the general script tradition which now is recognizable as the national script of the Ammonites (though it perhaps more accurately should be called the regional script of Transjordan, with McCarter 1980: 50). The language of Deir ʿAllā requires closer examination than it can be given here. Carlton's work on it is the best to date. Further research is needed with regard to the linguistic relationships between Deir ʿAllā and the other languages of the region, including Ammonite.

CHAPTER TWO
THE AMMAN CITADEL INSCRIPTION

Introduction

One of the most important West Semitic epigraphic finds of recent years is the 9th-century-B.C. Amman Citadel inscription. This stone inscription, 24 x 19 cm, was first discovered in 1961 but was not published until several years later, when Siegfried Horn brought it to light (1967–68: 81–83; 1969: 2–13). I will not discuss in this study the technical data concerning its history, archeological context, and present whereabouts, all of which are treated in Horn's article. F. M. Cross has dealt adequately with the problems of paleography, dating, and the historical implications of the text (1969a: 13–19). He also included a translation. Since the original publication, new readings and widely varying interpretations have been offered by Albright (1970: 38–40), Palmaitis (1971: 119–26), Garbini (1972: 103–8), Kutscher (1972: 27–28), Veenhof (1972: 170–79), Puech and Rofé (1973: 531–46), Dion (1975: 32–33), van Selms (1975: 5–8), Shea (1979: 17–25), Sasson (1979: 117–25), and Shea, again (1981: 105–10). The differing translations of these authors graphically illustrate the enigmatic nature of the inscription. Recently, W. J. Fulco published a new collation of the text, based on his "many days of studying the stone itself, under every possible lighting, at the Amman Archaeological Museum" (Fulco 1978: 41). Generally speaking, Fulco's readings of individual letters may be considered more accurate than those of the other scholars mentioned above, who worked primarily from photographs or, in Horn's case, from a squeeze. My study is based for the most part on Fulco's readings.

The aim of this study is to offer a new translation which makes sense of the inscription as a whole. I believe that it has a demonstrable pattern of thought and subject matter which flows through the entire text. However, recognizing the many difficulties of the inscription, resulting both from its fragmentary condition and our limited experience with the Ammonite language, I present this interpretation with due caution.

Text

1. m]lkm . bnh . lk . mb’t . sbbt[
2.] . kkl . msbb ‘lk . mt ymtn[
3.]kḥd . ’kḥd wkl . m‘rb[
4.]wbkl . sd̊rt ylnn ṣdq̊[m
5.]l . tdltbdlt . bṭn kbh[
6.]h . tšt‘ . bbn . ’lm [
7.]wš[ ]h . wn[
8.]šlm . lk . wš[lm

Translation

1. Mi]lkom, build for yourself entrances around [
2.] like anyone who surrounds you, they will surely die [
3.] I will surely annihilate. And anyone who causes [evil (?)] to enter [
4.] and in every hall (?), the just will dwell [
5.
6.] You shall fear the gods [
7. and
8.] peace for you and pe[ace

General Comments

A major problem presented by the Citadel inscription is the condition of the stone itself. It is obvious that what is now extant is not the complete text. The broken edges on both sides and the deliberate removal of the right bottom corner make it clear that we are dealing only with a fragment of what originally had been a larger inscription. Some relevant questions, of course, concern how much of the original we have and how much is missing on either side. These are important issues, because the larger the original inscription was, the less cohesive a context we should expect from the extant lines. From a smaller inscription, on the other hand, we should expect more sequence from one line to the next, since a greater percentage of the original would remain.

It can be noted in the translation that the text seems to deal with several different topics in a few short lines. If the original did not extend far to either side, then this would be somewhat out of the ordinary, though not impossible. But there is a faint thread of vocabulary and subject matter which runs through the narrative and binds the thought patterns together. Even so, it is clear that a certain amount of connecting material is missing which would be necessary for the transition from one line to the next. Because both sides contain fragmentary words, it is impossible to determine which side originally extended farther. But there is no question as to the fact that the stone originally extended to some extent in both directions. My conclusion, based mainly on the content of the text (see the discussion of line 1, below), is that the inscription as we now have it may represent as little as half of the original. It is perhaps too speculative to state more than this.

There is no way from our present information to posit how far the text extended vertically beyond line 8, if at all. However, it is clear from the blank space at the top of the stone, in which there is ample room for another line of text, that line 1 of our fragment was indeed the first line of the original.

It is essential for the interpretation of the text and the understanding of its overall meaning and purpose to identify its genre. The stone was found at the site of the Iron Age citadel of Rabbath-Ammon, the ancient Ammonite capital (Horn 1969: 2). Even in its present fragmentary condition, it is fairly large, and the content gives the impression that it was meant to be seen by many. Consideration of the vocabulary of lines 1, 4, and possibly 5, also sheds light on the purpose of the text. Line 1 contains the verbal form *bnh*, "build," followed by the architectural term *mb't*, "entrances." Line 4 contains *sdrt*, also an architectural term (see discussion below). These data, and other information in the text, suggest that it be classified as a monumental building inscription.

The first fragmentary word of the text appears to be part of a name, which is an important element of an introduction. Its syntactical function in the introductory phrase is vital for identifying who the speaker is, to whom he is speaking, and so forth.

These factors, in turn, establish to a great extent how the remainder of the text is understood. The name Milkom (if that reading of the first word is correct) and its relationship to the rest of the text—especially the first line—is a key to the reading of the entire inscription.

It is of major importance for the interpretation of any inscription to determine who the speaker is and to whom the words are addressed. The Citadel inscription presents problems in this respect because of the variety of verbal forms used and the apparent change of subject in each of the individual sentences. Note the following changes of subject. Line 1 contains the name Milkom, the subject of a verb which has been broken off from the left side of the inscription. The next verb in the line, *bnh*, is a 2nd person imperative. Line 2 has a 3rd person pl. subject. Line 3, which contains portions of two sentences, has a 1st person sg. subject and a 3rd person sg. subject. Line 4 has a 3rd person pl. subject. The final legible line, line 6, has as its subject a 2nd person. In spite of this wide range of verbs, it is my conclusion that after the initial *m]lkm* there is only one speaker for the remainder of the text, namely the Ammonite god Milkom. What is missing from the first line is perhaps something like "The words of Milkom," "Milkom said to me," or "Milkom commanded me" (see the discussion below). From that point on, beginning with the imperative *bnh*, Milkom is the sole speaker. The person to whom the words are addressed is the speaker of "*m]lkm*" and whatever preceded it. That same speaker is also the subject of the verb in line 6 and the "you" in lines 1, 2, and 8. It is probably safe to assume that this individual was an Ammonite king, who received instructions from his god Milkom to conduct the project of building the entrances, as stated in line 1, and possibly even parts of the citadel or even a temple.

I interpret the text as being the deity's command to build (line 1), his curse against those who act hostilely toward the king or defile the structures built at his command (lines 2, 3), and his blessings promised for the structures and those who frequent them (line 4). Line 5 possibly contains architectural instructions or specifications. Line 6 appears to be a mild warning—probably not aimed toward Milkom's enemies but toward the king or his people.

Philological Comments

Line 1

m]lkm: Milkom, the chief god of the Ammonites (1 Kgs 11:5; 2 Kgs 23:13; etc.). The three preserved letters could be (a) part of the deity's name, (b) part of the theophoric name of the author, or (c) part of a theophoric element in a patronymic. As names are a regular feature in the first line of inscriptions and identify either the speaker or the primary actor of the narrative, the identification of *m]lkm* is crucial for the interpretation of the rest of the text. I read *m]lkm* as the name of the deity himself. Fulco, who also identifies *m]lkm* with the Ammonite god, has suggested that the word belongs to a previous clause. In his view, the subject of *bnh* (a 3ms perfect) is an understood "Milkom" (Fulco 1978: 42). This leaves us with the situation in which the god Milkom builds something, which I consider unlikely. Van Selms (1975: 8) also reads Milkom as the subject, ". . . m]ilkom has built . . . ," as does Shea (1979: 18).

It is not impossible that *m]lkm* is the subject of *bnh*. In Biblical Hebrew the verb usually precedes the subject. The reverse order (subject + verb) is used, among other reasons, to show emphasis, contrast, or indicate a change of subject (Williams 1976: 96–98). I find it unlikely that a change of subject is taking place at this early point in the Citadel text or that the subject + verb syntax is needed to demonstrate contrast or emphasis. From a syntactical perspective, this word order is more often indicative of a new paragraph within a continuous narrative and is therefore not to be expected in an introductory phrase (Andersen 1966: 82–84).

I propose that Milkom is the subject of a clause now lost from the inscription, "*'mr ly*" or something similar. What follows then are the words of Milkom, which continue throughout the remainder of the inscription. If this reconstruction is correct, then the original text probably extended at least 10 cm farther before the word Milkom. If the inscription began with an introductory formula, identifying the author, then the original was still larger. In either case, we must be dealing with an inscription of considerable length.

bnh: **banɛ̄h* (or **banēh*), *Qal* imv 2ms from *bny*, "build." This command begins the direct address of Milkom. The Meša' inscription contains three sentences which are very similar in structure to the first line of the Citadel inscription and employ an imperative in the same manner. In line 14 we find *wy'mr ly kmš lk 'ḥz 't nbh*, "and Kemoš said to me, 'Go, seize Nebo.'" Similarly, we read in line 32, *wy]'mr ly kmš rd hltḥm*, "and Kemoš said to me, 'Go down, fight.'" In both of these sentences the pattern is identical to that which I have proposed for line 1 of the Citadel inscription: *wy'mr ly* + name of deity + imperative (beginning one or a series of commands). Another sentence from the Meša' inscription (lines 24–25) has a similar construction, but the king is the speaker, addressing his people: *w'mr lkl h'm 'šw lkm 'š br bbyth*, "and I said to all the people, 'Make for yourselves each one a cistern at his house.'" Of note in this sentence is the use of the imperative followed by the construction *l* + 2nd person pronoun, denoting for whom the action is performed. The same sequence is found in the present line, *bnh lk*.

The final *he* is a *mater lectionis* for ɛ̄ (or for *ē*; cf. the discussion of *'bnh*, AT 1, in chap. 4).

lk: probably **lak*, preposition *l* + 2ms suffix. For the vocalization, cf. Cross and Freedman 1952: 53, 65–67, and the discussion under Phonology and Orthography, below.

mb't: Biblical Hebrew *mĕbô'ōt*, "entrances." In the Hebrew Bible this term is masculine. The only occurrence of the word with the feminine plural suffix *-ōt* is found in Ezek 27:3. There is no reason to assume that the feminine plural suffix was not standard for this noun in Ammonite. The Tell Siran inscription (line 7) preserves a similar variant from Hebrew gender where the *-ōt* suffix is attached to *ywm*, "day" (very uncommon in Hebrew; only Deut 32:7; Ps 90:15). The attributive adjective which modifies *ywmt* in that case (*rbm*) bears the masculine suffix *-īm* (cf. the philological comments to TS 7, chap. 3). From what little context we have in this inscription, it appears that the text commemorates the building of these entrances, since that is all for which we have specific reference in Milkom's command. Perhaps other things were mentioned also.

sbbt: preposition, "around." The corresponding Biblical Hebrew form, *sĕbîbôt*, is a feminine plural from the noun *sābîb*, used as a preposition (*BDB*: 686–87). It modifies a noun which follows it or a pronominal suffix attached to it (cf. Num 11:24; Judg 7:18; 1 Sam 26:5). This interpretation agrees with that of Albright but differs from those of Cross and Fulco, who interpret *sbbt* as a noun—"courts" (Cross 1969a: 18) and "precinct" (Fulco 1978: 41). The Biblical Hebrew examples of nonverbal *sbb* are only rarely substantives; its use as an adverb or a preposition is much more common (*BDB*: 686–87). Our *sbbt* in line 1 modifies whatever was written after it, now lost from the stone. It undoubtedly was some kind of structure, possibly the citadel or a sanctuary.

Line 2

kkl: "like anyone." I read the initial *kap* as the preposition "like, as, according to." It is less likely to represent the conjunction *kî* affixed to *kl* (*contra* Fulco 1978: 42). In Moabite and Epigraphic Hebrew, *kî* is spelled consistently with the final vowel letter *yod*. There is no confusion between this and the prepositional morpheme *k*-, which always is written proclitically as in our example here. In contrast, *kî* always stands alone; i.e., it is not proclitic. In Biblical Hebrew, where hundreds of examples of both *kî* and *k*- are found, the distinction between them is clear; the conjunction stands as an independent word, and the final *yod* is written (*BDB*: 453–55, 471–75). In Ugaritic, however, *kî* is sometimes written proclitically (Gordon 1965: 107). The evidence from Phoenician is inconclusive, since vowel letters are not used and word dividers or word-dividing spaces are rare and inconsistent. Although it is unwise to make definitive statements concerning Ammonite orthography on the analogy of systems used for other languages, the evidence does seem to suggest that *k*- in the Citadel inscription is the preposition, attached to the following word.

msbb: *Po'el* participle, ms.

kl followed by a participle usually introduces a hypothetical situation, as in the following examples: *kol-mōṣ'î*, "anyone who finds me" (Gen 4:14), and *kol-hōrēg qayin*, "if anyone kills Cain"

(Gen 4:15; cf. also *BDB*: 482; 1 Sam 3:11; 2 Sam 5:8). Since participles are verbal nouns, *kl* followed by a singular indeterminate participle is translated as *kl* in conjunction with any singular indeterminate noun, "any, each, every" (*GKC*: #127*b*). In the present line, the best translation is "like anyone who surrounds you."

ʿlk: preposition *ʿl* + 2ms suffix *-k*. Fulco's examination of the stone convinced him that the hole before the *lamed* is the letter *ʿayin* with some of the stone inside the circle chipped out, rather than a word divider (1978: 41). Of importance for the semantics of line 2 is the use of the verb *sbb* in conjunction with the preposition *ʿl*. *mt ymtn*, which ends the line in a threatening tone, suggests that *sbb* here be interpreted in the same fashion. The Hebrew Bible uses *sbb* quite often with the sense of surrounding with hostile intentions. In 2 Kgs 6:15 it is used of an army surrounding a city in siege: *wĕhinnēh-ḥayil sôbēb ʾet-hāʿîr*. In Judg 20:5, *sbb* is used with the preposition *ʿl* in the context of surrounding a house and treating its inhabitants with violence: *wayyāsōbbû ʿālay ʾet-habbayit lāylâ*. In 2 Chr 18:31 a similar situation is described, also with *ʿl*: *wayyāsōbbû ʿālāyw lĕhillāḥēm*. I interpret line 2 of our inscription as being part of Milkom's curse against those who hostilely surround his king and his building project. The first three words belong to a subordinate clause of which they alone remain. The following phrase, *mt ymtn*, forms the main clause.

mt ymtn: **mōt yamūtūn*, *Qal* infinitive absolute + 3mpl imperfect from the hollow verb *mwt* (cf. *môt tāmût*, Gen 2:17). This was first identified correctly by Cross (1969a: 18). The emphatic infinitive + imperfect construction (*GKC*: #113*n*) is significant here because of the fact that it occurs again in the next line (see discussion below). Also noteworthy is the final *nun* on *ymtn*. This is the so-called *nun paragogicum*, which in Ugaritic, Aramaic, and to a limited degree in Hebrew and Phoenician, distinguishes the imperfect from the jussive in most 3rd person plural forms (Bauer and Leander 1922: #56*i*; Gordon 1965: 154; *GKC*: #47*m*; Harris 1936: 40). It is regular in Ammonite, at least as far as we can tell from the extant inscriptions; it is used in both of the plural imperfects attested, the one under discussion here and *ylnn* in line 4.

Line 3

]kḥd 'kḥd: infinitive absolute + 1cs imperfect from the verb *kḥd*. I prefer to read these as *Hip'ils*, since the *Hip'il* meaning of *kḥd*, "to cut off, destroy, annihilate," fits best in the context of the text. In Biblical Hebrew, the infinitive of the causative stem begins with the prefix *he*, which, though absent in our inscription, possibly was broken off immediately before the *kap*. In Phoenician there is an example of a compound where the *Qal* stem was used for the infinitive and the *Yip'il* was used for the imperfect: *wrgz trgzn* (*KAI* 13.7, Sidon, 6th century). The same phenomenon exists in Biblical Hebrew; e.g., *'a'alkā gam-'ālōh*, Gen 46:4 (cf. *GKC*: #113*w*). We may have a similar situation in *]kḥd 'kḥd*, but most likely there originally was a *he*, which was broken off when the stone was damaged.

wkl m'rb: "And anyone who causes [ ] to enter." This begins a new sentence. Fulco (1978: 41) is certain of the letters in the final word, which was read *m'r[.]b* by Cross (1969a: 17), Kutscher (1972: 27), and Dion (1975: 32), and *m'rk[t* by Albright (1970: 38). Note the *kl* + participle syntax; cf. *kl msbb* in line 2. The verb *'rb* is found also in Ugaritic (Gordon 1965: 461); it is a cognate of the Akkadian verb *erēbu*, "to enter." *BDB* (787) lists this as the verb which underlies the Biblical Hebrew noun *'ereb*. The semantic range of *erēbu* extends from entering by means of violent invasion to the entering of new months (*CAD* E: 259). The context of our inscription, which includes surrounding hostilely, dying, and being annihilated, supports an interpretation of *'rb* in an unfriendly vein (cf. *CAD* E: 226–27 for examples of *erēbu* used for violent entry, invasion, etc.). *m'rb* is a ms participle. The *Hip'il* stem is to be preferred here over the *Pi'el*, which would look identical to it in this writing system. The direct object, which is missing off the left side of the stone, to the right in the transliteration, is probably a word such as "evil" or "corruption." Thus I interpret *wkl m'rb* as the beginning of a curse against all those who attempt to defile the area or edifice under discussion by bringing evil into it. Also of a threatening nature, consistent in this context, is Cross's plausible proposal, *m'r b*, "all who incite," from *'wr* (1969a: 18).

From a standpoint of the literary style of the Citadel inscription, the emphatic-infinitive and the *kl* + participle constructions discussed above are important. Professor Charles R. Krahmalkov, to whom I am indebted for much of the following discussion, brought the literary patterns of this text and their significance to my attention. The author of the text shows a pattern in his curse formulas of lines 2 and 3. The offenders are mentioned in the initial clause of the sentence, and the curse is pronounced at the end. Furthermore, where we have the offenders specified, in both cases the syntax is the same, *kl* + participle: *kkl msbb* (line 2) and *wkl m'rb* (line 3). The curses are pronounced similarly also, using the emphatic infinitive + imperfect construction: *mt ymtn* (line 2) and *]kḥd 'kḥd* (line 3). I read in lines 2 and 3 three sentences: (1) the entirety of line 2, including something which was broken off at the beginning of the line; *mt ymtn* ends the sentence. (2) A sentence which ends with the pronouncement *]kḥd 'kḥd*. In light of the syntax discussed above, it is possible that the initial clause contained *kl* + participle, specifying the transgressor against whom the curse is directed. (3) A sentence which begins with *wkl m'rb* and possibly ends with an emphatic curse. If this reconstruction is correct, we have a series of three syntactically similar curses in the first part of the inscription, directed at those who violate the king's building project undertaken at the command of Milkom.

Line 4

wbkl: "and in every" (*GKC*: #127*b*).

s̊drt: This could be a word deriving from the verb *sdr*, which means "arrange in order" (*BDB*: 690; cf. Akkadian *sadāru*, *AHw*: 1000; and Mishnaic Hebrew/Jewish Aramaic *sdr*, Jastrow 1886–1903: 958). Fulco has pointed out the corresponding Biblical Hebrew *śĕdērâ* (1 Kgs 6:9; note the *śin* for the original initial *samek*; see Blau 1970: 114–25), which also comes from an architectural context but whose meaning is dubious. Judging from the context in the Citadel inscription and the meaning of the root, our word *sdrt* may mean "row, chamber, hall, colonnade," or something else which implies symmetry, order, and arrangement. Jewish Aramaic *sidrâ*/*sidrā'* has among its meanings "colonnade, hall" (Jastrow 1886–1903: 959). Fulco (1978: 41) and Puech and Rofé (1973: 537) read *sdrt* as a feminine plural. In Biblical Hebrew, plurals following *kl* are consistently determined: either by means of the definite article, a following noun in construct, or a pronominal suffix (*GKC*: #125*a*; *BDB*: 481). The same is true in Phoenician, Epigraphic Hebrew, and Moabite. Our *s̊ďrt* meets none of these requirements for determination and is best read as a singular in a construct relationship with the preceding *kl*.

Feminine singular substantives in Ammonite end in *-t*, unlike Hebrew *-â* (cf. *gnt*, TS 4). This is consistent with Moabite (*KAI* 181.3, 26, 27) and Phoenician (Harris 1936: 58–59).

ylnn: **yalīnūn*, "(they) will dwell," *Qal* imperfect 3mpl from *lyn*. Fulco's identification of the letters yields a word which makes excellent sense in its context. The verb *lyn* usually has the meaning "pass the night, lodge," indicating a temporary station overnight. However, the Bible preserves examples of the verb used in a less restrictive sense, meaning "abide, dwell, remain" (Prov 15:31; Job 19:4; in Job 39:28 it is used parallel with *škn*). Note Job 41:14: *bĕṣawwā'rô yālîn 'ōz*, "in his neck strength dwells," and Job 19:4: *'ittî tālîn mĕšûgātî*, "my error remains with me." For the final *nun*, which is consistent in our Ammonite evidence, see the discussion of *ymtn* (line 2), above. Consistent also with the other evidence from this inscription is the absence of *matres lectionis* indicating internal vowels.

ṣdq̊[m: "just (ones)." The possible *qop* is quite uncertain (Cross 1969a: 18; Fulco 1978: 40–41). Since this word ends with the break in the stone, we cannot determine without question whether any letters followed the proposed *qop*. Assuming that the *qop* is correct, the number of the preceding verb would suggest that a *mem* be restored, resulting in the plural *ṣdqm*, here used nominally (Biblical Hebrew *ṣadîqîm*; cf. Exod 23:8; Deut 16:19; etc.). Line 4 is translated, "and in every hall, the just will dwell."

Line 5

This is the most difficult line of the text, though almost all of the letters are clear and their identification is nearly certain. One point of disagreement among the commentators with respect to letter identification is the second-to-last letter of the line. This is identified as a *reš* by all of the authors listed in the introduction with the exception of Puech and Rofé and Fulco, who read a *bet*. Fulco's published transcription (1978: 41) incorrectly shows *reš* rather than *bet*, yet both his translation and his philological notes show that he reads *bet*. In a personal communication he confirmed to me that the *bet* is clear and unmistakable. Palmaitis reads a *bet* for the third letter of the line, against the otherwise unanimously accepted *dalet*. The word dividers are clear, but only two are found in the entire line of 15 letters, leaving us the unlikely combinations *tdltbdlt* and *bṭnkbh*. Because of the problems of this line, I have not been able to make a translation that I can consider satisfactory and thus will not propose a reading here.

The following are all of the published translations which were available to me:

Albright:

> [. . . and every]thing shalt thou inscribe on the terebinth board—invite (the army) to a feast [. . .]

Cross:

> . . . door by door. The bowl of its laver . . .

Dion:

> . . . tu inscriras sur la tablette de térébinthe. Un festin . . .

Fulco:

>]L. there will hang from its doors an ornament KBH[

Horn:

> . . .] door, at the inner door he dug [. . .

Kutscher:

> 't hdlt bdlt

Palmaitis:

> . . .] (?) extermination. In the passage which I chiseled through [. . .

Puech:

>] tu [ne] passeras *pas* par la porte de l'intérieur *car* l'effro[i . . *kbh*[*lh* . .

Rofé:

>] tu [ne] passeras *pas* par la porte de Beṭon parce que là [a passé] sa [pré]sence. *kbh*/[*dlt p*]*ṅh*

Sasson:

> fire devour]ing the innermost door [that will not] be quenched.

van Selms:

> [and he pla]nted the inner door inside; he dug . . .

Shea:

> . . . . portal-by-portal inward he dug . . . . .

I do not consider it necessary to address myself to each of these translations individually; however, a few observations are in order.

The initial *taw* of *tdltbdlt* has been interpreted by van Selms (1975: 8) and Kutscher (1972: 27) as the *nota accusativi*, written proclitically with the following noun. The same particle is written *'ēt*/*'et* in Biblical Hebrew, *'t* in Moabite, *'yt* in Phoenician, and *t*- in Punic (*PPG*²: #255). It is also written *t*- (alongside *'t*) in the 2nd-century-A.D. Hebrew documents from Wâdī Murabba'ât (Milik 1961: 291, and references there). Milik (1953: 284) explains the form *tšmym* (= Biblical Hebrew *'ēt haššāmayim*) as resulting from (a) the elision of *'alep* and (b) *t* + definite article *h*-, yielding an aspirated *t*. The Punic particle *t*- developed in unstressed proclitic position after the loss of the consonantal value of *'alep* (*PPG*²: #94).

Though the argument for our Ammonite *t*- being the *nota accusativi* is attractive, it is very unlikely. There is no evidence for *'alep* losing its consonantal value in this period. Moreover, *'t* and its equivalents occur several times in the contemporary Meša' inscription and elsewhere in South Canaanite writing throughout the history of the language. Unfortunately there are no examples of the *nota accusativi* in other Ammonite inscriptions. Finally, identifying *t-* in this manner does not solve the rest of the problems of the line.

Excising the initial *taw* of *tdltbdlt* (see above), van Selms (1975: 6) translates the remaining cluster, "inner door." There are several occurrences in the Hebrew Bible of *ḥeder bĕḥeder*, with the meaning "inner room" (rather than "a room within a room," or the like; 1 Kgs 20:30; 22:25; 2 Kgs 9:2). On the analogy of this construction, he reads "inner door" for *dltbdlt* and suggests that the scribe considered this expression to be one word, hence no word divider. This is plausible and probably is the best interpretation proposed thus far, but it does presuppose that the initial *taw* be considered a *nota accusativi*, a dittography (Fulco 1978: 42), or that it be removed in some other manner.

I find all attempts to identify verbal constructions in *tdltbdlt* unconvincing.

The word *bṭn* in line 5 is also problematic, although it is a common noun in Biblical Hebrew with the meaning "belly, womb." Our context makes such a translation difficult, though certainly not impossible. The same word appears as the name of an object of uncertain description in the narrative of the construction of Solomon's temple, 1 Kgs 7:20. It is not used as an adverb.

I have examined all of the proposed translations of line 5 carefully, and I concede that many of the suggested interpretations are possible. Yet given the complexity of the problems which need to be solved in it, I cannot offer any definitive solutions.

Line 6

*tšt*ʿ: "You shall fear," *Qal* imperfect 2ms from *št*ʿ. Cf. Phoenician: *yšt*ʿ and *nšt*ʿ*m*, *KAI* 26.AII.4 (Karatepe, 8th century). The same word is found in Ugaritic: *ṯt*ʿ, *UT* 49.VI.30 and *UT* 67.II.7, in both cases parallel to *yr*ʾ, "to fear." This verb is not attested in Biblical Hebrew (unless the form discussed below was pointed incorrectly by the Massoretes). Instead, a *Hitpa*ʿ*el* of *š*ʿ*y* is preserved, with metathesis of *šin* and *taw*, yielding *tšt*ʿ (= *tištā*ʿ; Isa 41:10). The verb *š*ʿ*y* means "to look/gaze around"; in the intensive-reflexive conjugation used in Isa 41:10, it has the sense of gazing around in anxiety or fright. This also is used in parallel construction with *yr'*. I find both the Phoenician/Ugaritic *št'*/*ṯt'* and the Biblical Hebrew tD *š'y* acceptable options for the identification of Ammonite *tšt'*. If we accept the former, our line is translated "You shall fear the gods." From the latter we get "You shall look in fear at the gods."

bbn 'lm: The initial *bet* is the preposition. The way it is translated depends on the translation of the preceding verb *tšt'*. If we take *tšt'* as a tD of *š'y*, then *b-* is rendered into English as "at." According to *BDB* (90, IVd), the preposition *b-* is used "with verbs expressive of sensible perception, to denote the . . . attentive exercise of the faculty concerned, as *šāma' bĕ* to listen *to*, *hibbîṭ bĕ*, *rā'â*, *ḥāzâ*, to look *upon*, *hērîaḥ bĕ* to smell *at*." This is precisely the usage which we have here in *tšt' b-*, "You shall look in fear at. . . ." Assuming that *tšt'* is from the root *št'*, we have two possible renderings for the following *b-*: (1) "Among": The preposition *b-* often has this sense when affixed to plural nouns; cf. *baqqōšĕrîm*, "among the conspirators" (2 Sam 15:31), and *bā'ănāqîm*, "among the giants" (Josh 14:15). (2) It is possible to render *tšt' b-* into English without translating the *b-*. Some verbs regularly take *b-* attached to the direct object; others do so sporadically (*BDB*: 90, IV). The Biblical Hebrew verb *yr'*, which appears to have the same meaning as Ammonite *št'*, is attested with *b-* affixed to its object in Jer 51:46: *wĕtîrĕ'û baššĕmû'â hannišma'at bā'āreṣ*, ". . . and you fear the report which is heard in the land."

bn 'lm: "gods," common in Ugaritic (Gordon 1965: 373), Phoenician (*KAI* 26.AIII.19, Karatepe, 8th century), and Biblical Hebrew (Gen 6:2, 4; Ps 29:1; 89:7; etc.; cf. Dion 1975: 31, n. 45). Of importance for the study of Ammonite orthography is the absence of a *mater lectionis yod* representing the final *-ē* on the mpl cstr *bn*. This consonantal spelling is consistent with Phoenician orthography but not with the systems used in contemporary Moabite, Hebrew, or Aramaic inscriptions, where long vowels in final position are written (Sherman 1966: 231). The same word is found written the same way in TS 1, 2, and 3, and in AT 2. The Tell Siran inscription also preserves another mpl cstr without final *yod*. Cf. the orthographic commentary below and the philological and orthographic notes in chap. 3, where this matter is discussed in greater detail.

There is a space after the word *'lm*. It is large enough for as many as two more letters. We can be reasonably sure, therefore, that *'lm* is a complete word. Note the mpl morpheme -*īm*, in contrast to -*īn*, which is used in the contemporary Meša' inscription.

Line 7

This line is too extensively damaged to permit any reading. Fulco has identified a *he* before a word divider in the center of the line. The *waw* which follows the word divider is most likely the conjunction "and."

Line 8

šlm lk: The first word may be cognate to the Biblical Hebrew noun *ă* ˆ
ing is the preposition + 2ms suffix, *lk*. I find the translation ". . . peace/well-being for you . . ." very attractive for a final line in this inscription, though we cannot be sure that line 8 is in fact the last line of the text. It is also possible that *]šlm* is a fragment of a different word.

Lexicon

'l	nm (6 = 'lm, pl) god
b-	prep (4, 6) in, among
bn	nm (6 = pl cstr) son
bny	vb (1 = bnh, *Qal* imv ms) build
w-	conj (3, 4, 7bis, 8) and
k-	prep (2) like, as, according to
kḥd	vb (3 = h]kḥd, *Hip'il* inf abs; 'kḥd, *Hip'il* impf 1cs) destroy, annihilate
kl	nm (2, 3, 4 = cstr) all
l-	prep (1, 8 = lk, l + 2ms sfx -k) to, for
lyn	vb (4 = ylnn, *Qal* impf 3mpl) dwell, remain
mb'(t)	n (1 = mb't fpl) entrance
mwt	vb (2 = mt, *Qal* inf abs; ymtn, *Qal* impf 3mpl) die
sbb	vb (2 = msbb, *Po'el* pcp ms) surround

sbbt	prep (1) around
sd̊rt	nf (4) chamber, hall, colonnade (?)
ʻl-	prep (2 = ʻlk, ʻl + 2ms sfx -k) upon
ʻrb	vb (3 = mʻrb, *Hipʻil* [?] pcp ms) enter (?)
ṣdq̊	nm (4 = ṣdq̊[m, mpl) just one, righteous one (?)
šlm	nm (8) completeness, well-being, peace
štʻ	vb (6 = tštʻ, *Qal* impf 2ms) fear

Divine Name

m]lkm (1)

Morphology

1. *Nouns*

a) Attested forms:

ʼlm (6)	mpl
bn (6)	mpl cstr
kl (2, 3, 4)	ms cstr
mbʼt (1)	fpl
sd̊rt (4)	fs (?)
ṣdq̊[m (4)	mpl (?)
šlm (8)	ms

b) Inflections:

ms:	šlm	-∅
ms cstr:	kl	-∅
mpl:	ʼlm	-m (-īm)
mpl cstr:	bn	-∅ (-ē)
fs:	sd̊rt (?)	-t (-at)
fpl:	mbʼt	-t (-ōt)

2. *Verbs*

a) Attested forms:

bnh (1)	*Qal* imv ms
h]kḥd (3)	*Hipʻil* inf abs (perhaps *Qal*?)
ʼkḥd (3)	*Hipʻil* impf 1cs (perhaps *Qal*?)
ylnn (4)	*Qal* impf 3mpl
mt (2)	*Qal* inf abs
ymtn (2)	*Qal* impf 3mpl
msbb (2)	*Poʻel* pcp ms

m'rb (3)	*Hip'il* pcp ms
tšt' (6)	*Qal* impf 2ms

b) Conjugations:

Qal

imperfect:

2ms	tšt'	t - - -
3mpl	ymtn ylnn	y - - - n

imperative:

ms	bnh	- - -

infinitive absolute:

mt		- - -

Hip'il

imperfect:

1cs	'kḥd	' - - -

participle:

ms	m'rb	m - - -

Po'el

participle:

ms	msbb	m - - -

3. *Prepositions*

b-	(4, 6)
k-	(2)
l-	(1, 8)
sbbt	(1)
'l-	(2)

4. *Conjunction*

w- (3, 4, 7, 8)

5. *Pronominal Suffix*

2ms -k (1, 2, 8)

Summary

In addition to the items discussed in the philological commentary above, the following notes concerning morphology are relevant:

a) *Nouns*: The morphology of the 9th-century Ammonite

noun is consistent with that of the other Ammonite texts and is generally consistent with that of the other Canaanite languages of the same time period, as evidenced by the inflectional terminations of number and gender: ms (-Ø), ms cstr (-Ø), mpl (*-īm*), mpl cstr (*-ē*), fs (*-at*), fpl (*-ōt*). The fs termination *-at* contrasts with *-â* (i.e., *āh*) of Judahite but agrees with Israelite and Moabite. Harris (1939: 38) suggests that Proto-Semitic had two forms, **-tu* and **-atu*, which alternated in different environments and which eventually were extended and leveled along geographical/dialectal lines. Judahite regularized **-atu*, which underwent the development **-atu* > **-at* > **-ā*. The other Canaanite dialects regularized **-tu*, which became **-t* with the loss of the final vowel. It is more probable that the Ammonite fs termination is **-at* (< **-atu*) and that the Judahite form results from the same development but with subsequent loss of the final *taw* (cf. Bauer and Leander 1922: #62*e–t*; *GKC*: #19*l*, 80*c*).

Ammonite contrasts with Moabite in its use of the mpl termination *-īm*. Moabite *-īn* stands alone against the rest of Canaanite but agrees with Aramaic.

The lack of a *yod* to represent the mpl cstr termination *-ē* is an orthographic, rather than a morphological, issue; cf. Phonology and Orthography, below.

b) *Verbs*: The morphology of the attested verbal forms is consistent with the other Canaanite languages, as demonstrated by the preformatives and afformatives: *Qal* imperfect 2ms: *t- - -*; *Qal* imperfect 3mpl: *y- - -n*; *Qal* imperative: Ø; *Qal* infinitive absolute: Ø; *Hip'il* imperfect 1cs: *'- - -*; *Hip'il* participle ms: *m- - -*; *Po'el* participle ms: *m- - -*.

Only the *Qal* imperfect 3mpl requires discussion. As I noted in the discussion of *ymtn* (line 2), the final *nun* is the *nun paragogicum*, which is used regularly in the imperfects of Ugaritic and Aramaic and less frequently in Biblical Hebrew and Phoenician. Both occurrences of 3mpl imperfects in the Citadel inscription have the terminal *nun*, so from our present knowledge we can assume that it was the regular form. This contrasts with the epigraphic evidence of Judahite and agrees with Aramaic. Moabite is silent on this point, as no 3mpl imperfects are attested.

If my interpretation of *'kḥd* (line 3) as a *Hip'il* 1cs imperfect is correct, then the Ammonite imperfect of the causative stem differs from that of Aramaic, which would retain the *he* after the preformative *'alep*.

c) *Prepositions*: The Citadel inscription shows evidence for the same types of prepositions used throughout Canaanite. Prefixed: *b-*, *k-*, *l-*, *'l-*; free-standing *sbbt*.

d) *Conjunction*: *w-*, always proclitic.

e) *Pronominal Suffix*: The only pronoun preserved in the Citadel inscription is the suffix *-k*, which agrees with Moabite and epigraphic Judahite but contrasts with literary Hebrew (as found in parts of the Bible and in the poetic inscriptions from Khirbet Beit Lei).

Phonology and Orthography

bnh (1): probably **banɛ̄h*. The final *he* is a *mater lectionis* for ɛ̄ (or possibly ē); it is the only vowel letter in the inscription. *He* is used to represent ɛ̄ in Moabite (*yhwh*, *KAI* 181.18), Israelite (*ymnh*, *KAI* 188.3), and Judahite (*wzh*, Siloam, *KAI* 189.1; *nr'h*, Lachish, *KAI* 194.12, etc.). For the phonological developments which brought about the ɛ̄, cf. the discussion of *'bnh*, AT 1, in chap. 4.

lk (1): probably **lak*. Cross and Freedman (1952: 65–67) have pointed out that two dialectal variants of the 2ms suffix existed in Hebrew, *-kā* and *-k*. The former form is the more ancient, and it survived in elevated speech and in literature. Though rare in pre-Exilic epigraphic material, it is attested in a literary inscription from Khirbet Beit Lei (Cross 1970: 305, n. 11). The short suffix was a somewhat later development, brought about by apocope, i.e., assimilation of the final vowel to the juncture. It became standard in the spoken language. The Hebrew Bible preserves both traditions; the consonantal text preserves primarily the short form, but the Massoretic pointing has leveled the vocalization throughout most of the Bible to conform with the earlier pronunciation (Cross and Freedman 1952: 66). The inscriptional evidence overwhelmingly attests the predominance of the apocopated form.

The longer form with *-kā* cannot be ruled out, however. Perhaps a final vowel *ā* did exist on the suffix, which was not represented orthographically. This nonrepresentation of final *ā* may have been the accepted orthographic practice for the 2ms suffix (cf. Ben-Ḥayyim 1954: 13–64). It is more likely, however, that the word *lk* was vocalized **lak*.

ʿlk (2): **ʿalēk*. For the suffix *k*, see *lk*, above; cf. *ʿlyk* in 11QPs[a] Zion 13, 14 (*DJD* 4: 87). The basic form of this preposition is **ʿalay* (Bauer and Leander 1922: #81*h*ʾ). Presumably this form was used with pronoun suffixes, while the shortened form **ʿal* was used in free-standing position. The orthography here indicates that the diphthong at the end of the preposition had contracted in Ammonite by the time its spelling was fixed: *ay* > *ē*. Had it not, the diphthong would be represented by *yod* in the orthography. The *ē* is not represented orthographically. This phonological development had taken place also in Israelite (*qṣ*, Gezer, *KAI* 182.7; *yn*, Samaria, *KAI* 185.3; 187.1; etc.), Moabite (*wbbth*, *KAI* 181.7; *ymh*, *KAI* 181.8), Phoenician (*ʿlk*, Byblos, *KAI* 3.5; *bt*, Zinjirli, *KAI* 24.5), where both in internal and final positions the contraction *ay* > *ē* had occurred by the beginning of the 1st millennium (Harris 1939: 29–32). Diverging from this pattern is Judahite Hebrew, where the contraction of diphthongs took place at a much later date, and even then only in special situations (Harris 1939: 31). The Massoretic Text preserves the historical spelling with the *yod* representing the original diphthong *ay* and a *qāmeṣ* signifiying the archaic (literary) long form of the 2ms suffix: *ʿāleykā*. As further evidence for the contraction of *ay*, cf. *bn* (AC 6; AT 2; TS 1, 2, 3), *mʿbd* (TS 1), and *yn* (H 1.7, 8).

bn (6): **banē*. This word also appears spelled defectively in the Tell Siran inscription (TS 1, 2, 3) and in the Theater inscription (AT 2). These examples suggest strongly that it was spelled regularly by the scribes of Ammon without the final vowel sound *ē* being represented in the orthography. The same phenomenon is observed also in the mpl cstr *mʿbd* (TS 1). In contrast, we do know that Ammonite scribes represented other final vowels with *matres lectionis* (e.g., *bnh*, AC 1; *ʾbnh*, AT 1; probably also *ʿlyh*, AS 52). Cf. the discussion of *bn* in the orthographic notes in chap. 3.

lk (8): See discussion of *lk* (1), above.

Summary

a) No internal vowels are represented in the orthography by *matres lectionis* (with Phoenician, Moabite, Israelite, and Judahite).

b) Final ē is represented by *he* (*bnh*, line 1) (with Moabite, Israelite, and Judahite).

c) The contraction *ay* > *ē* had taken place in Ammon by the 9th century (with Phoenician, Moabite, and Israelite; against Judahite).

d) Final *ē* (< *ay*) is not represented orthographically (with Phoenician; against Judahite and Moabite).

e) The 2ms suffix appears in its apocopated form, *-k* (with Moabite and epigraphic Judahite; against literary Hebrew; no data available for Israelite; Phoenician evidence is ambiguous).

From the limited body of orthographic information preserved in the Citadel inscription, we can conclude tentatively that 9th-century Ammonite fits well within the mainstream of Canaanite of that period, both phonologically and orthographically. Orthographically, Ammonite agrees in all areas examined with nearby and contemporary Moabite, except in the spelling *bn* for **banē*. Also consistent with the mainstream of Canaanite, and contrary to the phonology of the Judahite dialect, is the fact that Proto-Canaanite *ay* had contracted to *ē* by the period of our inscription.

Word Division

Consistent with the practice of many of the scribes of other Northwest Semitic epigraphs (Naveh 1973: 206; Millard 1970: 5–8), the scribe of the Citadel inscription used marks to separate words. These are small dots near the upper portion of the letters, used regularly, but not with consistency. In his study of the use of word dividers and so-called *scripto continua*, A. R. Millard (1970: 15) has isolated the following general rules concerning the use of dividers in the Northwest Semitic writing traditions, some of which are applicable to Ammonite:

> Words are separated from each other except for
> (1) single-letter proclitic particles (e.g., *k*, *w*, *b*)
> (2) sometimes the *nota accusativi*
> (3) sometimes bound forms (construct + regnant noun, infinitive absolute + regnant verb)
> (4) sometimes the third person plural suffix

(1) The Citadel text is consistent in its proclitic writing of the particles *b*-, *k*-, *l*-, and *w*- (examples in every line except line 5). (2) There are no examples of the *nota accusativi*. (3) Millard's inclusion (1970: 7) of "infinitive absolute + regnant verb" is based in part on the two occurrences of this construction in the Citadel inscription. In the case of *]kḥd . 'kḥd*, however, it is based on Cross's incorrect transcription of the line, where the obvious word divider is omitted (Cross 1969a: 17). All of the construct chains in our inscription (*kkl . msbb*, line 2; *wkl . m'rb*, line 3; *wbkl . sdrt*, line 4; *bbn . 'lm*, line 6) are separated by word dividers. (4) No 3rd person plural suffixes are in our inscription. (Millard includes this in his list because of the appearance of *hm* separated from the verb *w'sḥb* in the Meša' inscription, line 18. This may be an independent pronoun, rather than a misplaced object suffix. Cf. Donner and Röllig 1962–64 II: 117; Segert 1961: 217–18, 236.)

I have isolated 25 locations in our text where we should predict the appearance of word dividers: at all word boundaries, excluding edges of the stone where letters are missing or where no room remains for a divider. The dividers are found in 18 of these locations, or in 72% of the expected places. Dividers are absent in:

> line 2: between *msbb* and *'lk*
> line 2: between *mt* and *ymtn*
> line 3: between *'kḥd* and *wkl*
> line 4: between *sdrt* and *ylnn*
> line 4: between *ylnn* and *ṣdq*
> line 5: somewhere in *tdltbdlt* (?)
> line 5: between *bṭn* and *kbh* (?)

I would identify all of these as scribal inconsistencies, since there appears to be no rational reason for them, and they exhibit no pattern. If the absence of a divider between *mt* and *ymtn* (line 2) is deliberate, then the divider between *]kḥd* and *'kḥd* (line 3) is unexplainable. Inconsistencies on the part of our scribe are not restricted to the representation of word dividers. The spacing is irregular, and, as Horn pointed out in the *editio princeps*, the size of the letters varies wildly: *lamed* varies from 12 to 20 mm; *kap* varies from 18 to 28 mm; *yod* varies from 10 to 15 mm; and *samek* varies from 13 to 26 mm (Horn 1969: 4). The scribe who left us this inscription was not as skillful as some of his counterparts elsewhere in the Near East.

Linguistic Affiliation of the Amman Citadel Inscription

The entire corpus of Ammonite epigraphic material from the 9th century is contained in the Amman Citadel inscription. There are no other inscriptions from this period. Of the many Ammonite seals which have now been discovered, none can be dated earlier than the late 8th century (Herr 1978: 59–75). We possess, therefore, only one epigraph upon which to base our conclusions concerning the language and writing system used by the scribes of Ammon at that time.

The Amman Citadel inscription is written in a language that is demonstrably Canaanite, the same language found in the other texts discussed in this study. The following brief synopsis is a summation of material which already has been presented in detail. Most documentation has been omitted (for which see the commentaries of the individual items and the grammatical analyses, above).

Lexicon

There are nine recognizable nouns in the Citadel inscription, all of which are found in the Hebrew Bible. The word *sdrt* (line 4) is written with initial *śin* in 1 Kgs 6:9, but it is found spelled as in our text in Mishnaic Hebrew, a Canaanite dialect attested primarily from the early centuries A.D. (Segal 1927: 1–20).

Of the seven attested verbal roots, all are found in Canaanite: *bny*, *kḥd*, *lyn*, *mwt*, and *sbb* are attested abundantly in the Bible; *št'* is known from Phoenician; *'rb* is found in Ugaritic and in various nominal forms in Phoenician and Hebrew.

The five prepositions of the Citadel inscription are all well known from Canaanite, as is the conjunction *w*-. The only pronominal suffix represented here (-*k*, 2ms) is consistent throughout Northwest Semitic.

Morphology

The morphology of the Citadel inscription is identical to that of the other inscriptions classified as Ammonite. The inflectional terminations of the nouns and the preformatives and afformatives of the verbal conjugations are well in line with the other Canaanite dialects with which we are familiar (cf. the summary under Morphology, above). The mpl ending -*m* aligns Ammonite with Hebrew and Phoenician and against Moabite. The fs ending -*t* aligns Ammonite with Israelite, Phoenician, and Moabite and against Judahite.

Ammonite demonstrates regular use of the final *nun* on the 3mpl imperfect. This is found throughout Northwest Semitic but occurs consistently only in Ugaritic and Aramaic and now Ammonite.

Conclusion

The evidence presented throughout this entire chapter demonstrates that the 9th-century Ammonite of the Amman Citadel inscription is Canaanite—identical to the language of the other Ammonite inscriptions and with close affinities to the Hebrew of the Bible and to the other Iron Age dialects of Lebanon, Cisjordan, and Transjordan: Phoenician, Judahite, Israelite, and Moabite.

CHAPTER THREE
THE TELL SIRAN INSCRIPTION

Introduction

The Tell Siran inscription is the second longest complete Ammonite text. The only complete text which is longer is the Nimrud ostracon; both the Citadel inscription and H 1, which are fragmentary, are also longer than the Tell Siran text. It was written on a 10-cm-long bronze bottle in the Ammonite script, which was derived from the Aramaic script which the scribes of Ammon had adopted near the mid-8th century (Cross 1973a: 13; 1975: 12). Cross dates the text to about 600 B.C. (1973a: 14). The inscription was first published by H. O. Thompson and F. Zayadine in 1973 (1973a: 5–11; 1973b: 115–40; Thompson 1973: 7–8). Since that time, several other treatments of the text or notes to it have been published (Cross 1973a; Veenhof 1973; Thompson and Zayadine 1974; Dion 1975: 24–28; Krahmalkov 1976; Loretz 1977; Shea 1978; Becking 1981).

The identification of the letters in the inscription causes few problems, since most are preserved quite clearly. But full interpretation of the text is difficult because of two problematic words, *wh'tḥr* (line 4) and *w'šḥt* (line 5). The purpose of the bottle and its relationship to the inscribed text are also matters of some debate. Thompson and Zayadine (1973a: 10) see in the inscription a commemorative building text; Krahmalkov (1976: 55) views the existence of a building inscription on a little bottle as incongruous and proposes instead that the bottle and the text (a poem) together form one harmonious piece of art; Shea (1978: 107–8) refers to a wine-drinking song inscribed on what he suggests is a wine vessel. Each of these options is possible. The wide variety of the differing translations, including my own, reflects the difficulty and uniqueness of this puzzling text. The translation and discussion that follow should be considered in conjunction with the proposals published elsewhere.

In the commentary, I have discussed only items of orthographic or morphological interest and items which aid in the classification of Ammonite.

Text

1. m'bd 'mndb mlk bn 'mn
2. bn hṣl'l . mlk bn 'mn
3. bn 'mndb mlk bn 'mn
4. hkrm . wh . gnt . wh'tḥr
5. w'šḥt
6. ygl wyšmḥ
7. bywmt rbm wbšnt
8. rḥqt

Translation

1. The works of 'Ammīnadab king of the Ammonites
2. son of Hiṣṣīl'il king of the Ammonites
3. son of 'Ammīnadab king of the Ammonites:
4. the vineyard and the garden and the 'TḤR
5. and cisterns.
6. May he rejoice and be happy
7. for many days and in years
8. far off.

General Comments

The translations of Krahmalkov, Loretz, and Shea hinge upon (a) the use of the bottle and (b) the purpose of lines 4–8.

The first word of the inscription, *m'bd*, announces the nature of the items which are listed after the identification of their creator. It is in a construct relationship to 'Ammīnadab, who is presented here with his title and his ancestry back two generations. 'Ammīnadab's "works" (lines 4 and 5) are presented in apposition to *m'bd 'mndb*, without a copula.

Lines 6–8 comprise a wish or blessing formula, aimed toward 'Ammīnadab, possibly in honor of his accomplishments, including the works cited in the inscription.

The jar itself is somewhat enigmatic, though it does belong to a genre attested by other examples found in Jordan and Syria. Dr. James A. Sauer shared the following data with me. Its size and shape are exactly the same as those of small alabaster, pottery, and glass jars of the Neo-Babylonian and early Persian periods (the Tell Siran jar dates from the Neo-Babylonian period) which probably were used to contain spices or precious ointments. It does not resemble any large jar used for the storage of wine, nor would it have been used for drinking, due to its broad rim. Sauer concludes, "I would consider the object not to be related at all to wine, but rather to some other precious substance of small quantity." The actual contents of the jar itself also point away from a wine-drinking interpretation. When opened by its excavators, it was found to contain (a) grain, mostly barley, plus wheat and a few weed seeds, and (b) the unrecognizable remains of a very small copper object (Thompson and Zayadine 1973b: 118). The jar had been sealed by a metal lid which was secured in place by a bolt which ran through the lid and both sides of the jar and was hammered into rivets at both ends (Thompson and Zayadine 1973b: 117). The bolt was in place when the bottle was found.

This inscription is obviously not a monumental text in the normal sense of the term. Moreover, the relationship between the text and the object upon which it was incised is not clear—if any relationship was in fact intended. Nonetheless, the text is best read as commemorative, recognizing the works of the Ammonite king and offering a wish for his continued well-being.

Philological Comments

mʿbd (1): **maʿbadē*, "works of." This noun is attested only once in the Hebrew Bible (Job 34:25). It is interpreted by Krahmalkov (1976: 56) as a singular referring to the text itself and is translated "poem." Loretz (1977: 170) reads "Gegenstand" (= object), referring to the bottle: "*mʿbd* bezeichnet somit den beschrifteten Gegenstand selbst." Shea (1978: 108) reads "(The wine in this vessel comes) From the cultivation," identifying a noun *ʿbd* (work in an agricultural context, i.e., cultivation) plus the prefixed preposition *m-*. I suggest that the "works" of ʿAmmīnadab are the items listed in lines 4 and 5. This seems to be the most straightforward translation, though the identification of one of the items listed as his works (see below) is very difficult. *mʿbd* is plural, with the mpl cstr ending *-ē* unrepresented, consistent with the Ammonite orthography.

bn (1, 2, and 3): This can only be the mpl cstr (cf. the orthographic notes, below).

gnt (4): **gannat* (or **ginnat*; cf. Krahmalkov 1976: 56 and *GKC*: #27*s*). The Biblical Hebrew cognates are *gan*, the regular masculine noun, and *gannâ*, a feminine noun which appears less frequently. Note the fs afformative *-at*, in contrast to Biblical Hebrew *-â*. The ending *-at* is attested in feminine nouns elsewhere in Ammonite (*sdrt*, AC 4; *nkʾt*, H 1.4, 5) and is regular in Moabite (*KAI* 181.3, 26, 27) and Phoenician (Harris 1936: 58–59).

whʾtḥr (4): conjunction *w-* + def art *h-* + *ʾtḥr*, a noun of uncertain meaning. Contra Krahmalkov (1976: 56–57), Loretz (1977: 170), and Shea (1978: 108), I read this and the following word as nouns, the third and the fourth in the list comprising the "works of ʿAmmīnadab," since they seem to follow easily in that sequence and since the text becomes awkward when they are translated as verbs. *ʾtḥr* may be related to the Arabic words *maḥāra*^{tun} and *ḥāʾir*^{un}. The former derives from a root *ḥwr* and is translated "a thing in which water is collected" (Lane 1865: 667). *ḥāʾir*^{un}, "a place in which water collects," or "trough" (Lane 1865: 685), derives from *ḥyr*. The *ʾtḥr* may then be a surface pond of some sort, over against the *ʾšḥt*, probably underground cisterns.

wʾšḥt (5): conjunction *w-* plus a noun *ʾšḥt*. Thompson and Zayadine (1973a: 10) have translated this word as "cisterns," equating it with Moabite *ʾšwḥ* (*KAI* 181.9, 23). This is most probably correct, though there is no way to tell whether the Ammonite word is singular or plural. The Moabite word comes from a root similar or identical to Hebrew *šwḥ*, meaning (in Hebrew) "sink down" (BDB: 1001). The Biblical Hebrew cognate is *šûḥâ* (Jer 2:6). "Cisterns" fits well in the context, but the orthography of Ammonite *ʾšḥt vis-à-vis* Moabite *ʾšwḥ* makes equating them uncertain. If there are no internal *matres lectionis* in the Mešaʿ inscription, as has been suggested by Cross and Freedman (1952: 43), then the medial *waw* of the Moabite word, being part of the root, is certainly consonantal. Since Ammonite *ʾšḥt* lacks the *waw*, it may come from a different, though related, root or simply reflect a later stage in the history of the word. The Hebrew cognate lacks the prosthetic *ʾalep* of the Moabite and Ammonite examples. I have chosen to translate *ʾšḥt* as a plural only because it differs from the other listed works in that it has no definite article.

ywmt (7): "days." Note the fpl ending. This noun is masculine, as is shown by the mpl termination on the adjective which modifies it. In Biblical Hebrew, *yôm* regularly takes the plural ending *-īm*, but two examples of *yĕmôt* (< **yamōt*) are preserved (Deut 32:7; Ps 90:15). Cf. also *ymt* in *KAI* 4.5 and *KAI* 7.5, both in 10th-century Byblian Phoenician texts. For the spelling of this word, see the orthographic commentary below.

rbm (7): **rabbīm*. Note the mpl ending *-īm*.

šnt (7): **šanōt*, "years." In Biblical Hebrew, this word takes the mpl suffix *-īm*, though the cstr *šĕnôt* is used occasionally (Deut 32:7, etc.). *šnt* is the regular plural in Phoenician. It is not certain what the singular of this noun is in Ammonite. Biblical Hebrew has *šānâ* (< **šanat* < **šanatu*), but Moabite, Phoenician, and Israelite have *št*, i.e., **šat* (< **šant* < **šantu* < **šanatu*).

Lexicon

ʾšḥt	nf (5 = fpl) cisterns (?)
ʾtḥr	n (4) (?)
b-	prep (7) in, for
bn	nm (2, 3 = cstr; 1, 2, 3 = pl cstr) son
gyl	vb (6 = ygl, *Qal* juss 3ms) rejoice
gnt	nf (4) garden
h	def art (4 = h; 4bis = h-) the
w-	conj (4bis, 5, 6, 7) and
ywm	nm (7 = ywmt, fpl) day
krm	nm (4) vineyard
mlk	nm (1, 2, 3 = cstr) king
mʿbd	nm (1 = pl cstr) work
rb	adj (7 = rbm, mpl) many, much

rḥq	adj (8 = rḥqt, fpl) distant, far off
šmḥ	vb (6 = yšmḥ, *Qal* juss 3ms) be glad, be happy
š(n)t	nf (7 = šnt, fpl) year

Personal Names

hṣl'l	(2)
ʻmndb	(1, 3)

Place Name

ʻmn	(1, 2, 3)

Morphology

1. *Nouns and Adjectives*

a) Attested forms:

'šḥt (5)	fpl (?)
'tḥr (4)	ms (?)
bn (2, 3)	ms cstr
bn (1, 2, 3)	mpl cstr
gnt (4)	fs
ywmt (7)	fpl
krm (4)	ms
mlk (1, 2, 3)	ms cstr
mʻbd (1)	mpl cstr
rbm (7)	mpl
rḥqt (8)	fpl
šnt (7)	fpl

b) Inflections:

ms:	'tḥr (?)	-∅
	krm	-∅
ms cstr:	bn	-∅
	mlk	-∅
mpl:	rbm	-m (-īm)
mpl cstr:	bn	-∅ (-ē)
	mʻbd	-∅ (-ē)
fs:	gnt	-t (-at)
fpl:	'šḥt (?)	-t (-ōt)
	ywmt	-t (-ōt)

rḥqt	-t (-ōt)
šnt	-t (-ōt)

2. *Verbs*

a) Attested forms:

ygl (6)	*Qal* juss 3ms
yšmḥ (6)	*Qal* juss 3ms

b) Conjugations:

Qal

jussive:

3ms	ygl	y- - -
3ms	yšmḥ	y- - -

3. *Preposition*

b- (7)

4. *Definite Article*

h (4[tris])

5. *Conjunction*

w- (4[bis], 5, 6, 7)

Summary

The morphology of the Tell Siran inscription demonstrates its position among the Canaanite dialects.

a) *Nouns and adjectives*: The inflectional endings are generally consistent with those of Moabite, Judahite, and Israelite: ms (-∅), ms cstr (-∅), mpl (-*īm*), mpl cstr (-*ē*), fs (-*at*), and fpl (-*ōt*). Ammonite fs -*at* contrasts with Judahite -*â* but agrees with Israelite, Moabite, and Phoenician. The mpl ending -*īm* contrasts with Moabite -*īn*.

b) *Verbs, preposition, and conjunction*: These show no divergence from the patterns well known in other dialects.

c) *Definite article*: *h* appears three times in line 4, in one case separated from its noun by a word divider (see Word Division, below).

Phonology and Orthography

m'bd (1): **ma'badē*; *bn* (1, 2, 3): **banē*. These words are extremely important because they do not preserve an orthographic representation for the masculine plural construct ending -*ē*. The same phenomenon is found also in the word *bn* in the Citadel inscription (AC 6) and in the Theater inscription (AT 2). The contraction of the diphthong *ay* had taken place in Ammonite by this period, as is attested by the spelling *yn* for "wine" in H 1.7, 8 and by *'lk* (**'alēk* < **'alayk*) in AC 2. Furthermore, had the contraction not yet taken place, the diphthong *ay* would have been represented by its consonantal element *yod* in the words *bn* and *m'bd* under consideration here and in *bn* in the earlier Citadel text. This defective spelling of final -*ē* contrasts with the orthographic systems used in contemporary Aramaic, Moabite, and Hebrew, where long vowels in final position are represented (Sherman 1966: 231; for Arad, cf. Parunak 1978: 25–26). Cf. the orthographic comments to *bn* in the Citadel inscription, chap. 2.

ywmt (7): This word, with its unprecedented internal *waw*, is important orthographically and introduces a difficult problem in Canaanite phonology (cf. Cross and Freedman 1952: 24, 50, 53). It appears that early Canaanite possessed both **yam* and **yawm* as biforms for the word "day" (Freedman 1962: 97; cf. the contrasting view of Rainey 1972). In Biblical Hebrew the plural was constructed from **yam* (i.e., *yāmîm*), and **yawm* was used for the singular. With the contraction of *aw*, the form *yôm* resulted. In contrast, the Judahite inscriptions, which show no evidence of the contraction of *aw*, preserve *ym*, implying that the singular form in the epigraphs resulted from **yam*. In Ammonite it is likely that the plural used **yawm*, as our present *ywmt* contains an internal *waw*.

Unlike the contraction *ay* > *ē*, which in Ammonite is attested by *'lk* (AC 2), *yn* (H 1.7, 8), and mpl cstrs *bn* (AC 6; AT 2; TS 1, 2, 3) and *m'bd* (TS 1), there is no direct unambiguous evidence in the Ammonite corpus either for or against the contraction *aw* > *ō* having taken place by the time of our texts. Yet the presence of the internal *waw* in *ywmt* argues strongly that *aw* had not contracted. Harris wrote in 1939 (29–31) that the contractions *aw* > *ō* and *ay* > *ē* had taken place at an early time in all of Iron Age Canaanite except Judahite. The dialect of Ammon, since discovered, conforms to the pattern insofar as *ay* > *ē* is concerned. The evidence from the Meša' inscription (*KAI* 181) bears out Harris's conclusion with respect to Moabite (e.g., *hš'ny*, *KAI* 181.4; *w'šb*, *KAI* 181.13). If *aw* > *ō* took place in Ammonite close to the time when it did in Moabite (before 850 at the latest), or if *aw* > *ō* took place concurrently with *ay* > *ē* (as Harris implies, 1939: 29), then Ammonite *ywmt* would be vocalized **yômōt*, and the *waw* would be a historical spelling. The *waw* itself is ambiguous, since there is no way to determine whether it is a vowel letter which exists as a result of the retention of a historical spelling (i.e., the spelling *ywm* was fixed before *aw* > *ō*) or whether it represents the diphthong *aw*. The latter option is most likely; cf. Cross (1973a: 15). Cross maintains that in Ammonite *ay* had become *ē* and *aw* had remained uncontracted (personal communication).

Summary

a) The contraction *ay* > *ē* had taken place, as evidenced by the spelling of *m'bd* and *bn* (with Moabite, Phoenician, and Israelite; against Judahite).

b) Final -*ē* (< *ay*) is Ø in the orthography: *m'bd* (line 1) and *bn* (lines 1, 2, 3) (with Phoenician; but contra Hebrew and Moabite, where final vowels are represented generally in this period; unique to Ammonite).

c) The diphthong *aw* had not contracted to *ō*: *ywmt* (line 7) (with Judahite; against Moabite, Phoenician, and Israelite).

Word Division

The scribe of the Tell Siran inscription was not consistent in his use of word dividers. Only 3 of the 17 line-internal word boundaries are noted with dividing marks (cf. the discussion of word division in chap. 2, and Millard 1970: 15). In addition to the 3, there is a word divider separating an article from its noun, *wh . gnt* (line 4). There is no clear explanation for this, especially in light of the two other definite articles in the same line written proclitically. It is possible, however, that the scribe of this inscription viewed the definite article as a morpheme which was separable from the noun which followed it, much as prepositions and the conjunction *w* were sometimes separable in Ugaritic (Gordon 1965: 23).

Linguistic Affiliation of the Tell Siran Inscription

The language of the Tell Siran inscription is Ammonite, the language of the Amman Citadel inscription, the Amman Theater inscription, the Heshbon ostraca, the Nimrud ostracon, and numerous seals. It has close affinities to the other Canaanite dialects, Phoenician, Moabite, Israelite, and Judahite.

Lexicon

The Tell Siran inscription contains the difficult word *'tḥr* (line 4), which I read as a noun, as noted above. The word *'šḥt* has cognates in Moabite and Hebrew. Of the remaining lexical items, all are found in the Hebrew Bible. Moreover *bn*, *mlk*, and *šnt/št* are found in inscriptions from all dialects, *ywm/ym* is attested in all dialects but Israelite, *krm* is found only in Israelite, and *gyl*, *gn*, *m'bd*, *rḥq*, and *šmḥ* are otherwise unattested in Canaanite epigraphs (*DISO*; Donner and Röllig 1962–64 III: 1–26). It is likely that much of the distribution of words as attested by the small corpus of South Canaanite inscriptions can be attributed to the chances of discovery. As new discoveries are made in the future, we can expect the emergence of a clearer pattern of complementary distribution of lexical items among the dialects.

Morphology

As noted above, the morphology of the Tell Siran inscription demonstrates that Ammonite is a Canaanite dialect (cf. the discussion of morphology above and that of the Citadel inscription, chap. 2).

CHAPTER FOUR
THE AMMAN THEATER INSCRIPTION

Introduction

The Amman Theater inscription, a triangular stone fragment ca. 27 cm long and 5–17 cm wide, was discovered in 1961 during the excavation of the Roman theater at Amman. It was first published by R. Dajani in 1968 (1967–68: 65–67 and pl. 39). Soon thereafter, B. Oded treated it briefly (1969: 187–89). In 1975 F. M. Cross discussed the inscription, particularly with regard to its paleography (1975: 11–12). Recently a new photograph, a hand drawing, and a short treatment were offered by W. J. Fulco (1979: 37–38), which clarified some ambiguities in Dajani's study and proposed a different reading for one of the letters.

Cross orginally identified the script of the inscription as "cursive Aramaic" (in Thompson and Zayadine 1973a: 5, n. 2) and dated the text to ca. 580 B.C. (1975: 12) and later ca. 575 B.C. (1976: 148). Fulco concurs in general with those dates: "rather late, certainly after 600 B.C." (1979: 38).

Text and Translation

1.]b'l . 'bnh̊[	1.]-ba'al. I will build [
2.]bn 'm[n	2.] the Ammo[n]ites [

The *]b'l* in line 1 is part of the identification of the author, either his own name or that of his father. It could, however, be the title of the deity. The second word, *'bnh*, is a *Qal* impf 1cs of *bny*. Line 2 contains the combination *bn*, mpl cstr, and *'mn*; i.e., "the Ammonites," or "the people of Ammon."

Lexicon

bn nm (2 = pl cstr) son
bny vb (1 = 'bnh, *Qal* impf 1cs) build

Personal Name

-b'l (1)

Place Name

'm[n (2)

Morphology

The morphology of the noun and the verb found in this text does not differ in any way from that of the other examples in the Ammonite corpus.

Phonology and Orthography

The identification of *bn* as the mpl cstr further demonstrates the Ø spelling of *ē* < *ay* as seen in AC 6 and TS 1, 2, 3 (cf. Cross's comments on that subject, 1975: 12, n. 34).

The verb *'bnh* is also noteworthy, as it exhibits a *mater lectionis* for the final vowel. The vowel represented by *he* resulted from tone-lengthening in words which had *i* in certain positions in Proto-Canaanite. This tone-lengthening took place as the stress shifted from the first syllable of the word to the *i*, after the loss of the final vowel (Gibson 1966: 47; Harris 1939: 4, 60–61; *PPG*²: #72). The development of *'bnh* can be proposed as follows: Bronze Age Canaanite **'ábniu* > **'ábnī* > **'abnī́* > **'ibnɛ̄́* (Biblical Hebrew *'ebneh*; cf. Bauer and Leander 1922: #14*r*, *v*; 25*n'*; 57*c*).

Bergsträsser (1918: 117), Cross and Freedman (1952: 43, 57), Harris (1939: 4, 60), and Friedrich and Röllig (*PPG*²: #72) all vocalize tone-lengthened *i* as *ē* and make no graphic distinction between that sound and *ē* < *ay*. In contrast, Bauer and Leander distinguish between two sounds by using *ē* for the contracted diphthong *ay* and the symbol *ǣ* for tone-lengthened *i* (e.g., #57*c*; 73; cf. 64). Since Ammonite exhibits an orthographic distinction (see below), it is necessary to determine whether a phonemic distinction existed as well.

As was pointed out in the orthographic discussions of the other Ammonite inscriptions, the phoneme ē (< *ay*) probably was not represented in Ammonite spelling. Since the final vowel in *'bnh* is represented by *he* when ē (< *ay*) was Ø in the orthography, it can be argued that the vowel which resulted from tone-lengthening of *i* (which I will represent in the following discussion by ϵ̄) and ē which resulted from the contraction of *ay* were at one time, if not always, separate phonemes (cf. Cross and Freedman 1952: 38) and were treated as such in Ammonite orthography. The consonantal tradition preserved in the Masoretic Text, which distinguishes between the two sounds by the use of *yod* for ē and *he* for ϵ̄, seems to bear this out, at least as far as Hebrew is concerned. Furthermore, the Tiberian vocalization shows two separate sounds, generally using *segol* for ϵ̄ and *ṣere* for ē (for the evidence of the Babylonian vocalization, which shows no distinction, cf. Ben-Ḥayyim 1978: 95–96). Evidence from other Canaanite inscriptions also suggests a distinction between the two sounds. The phoneme ē is represented consistently either by *yod* or not at all (usually in medial position); ϵ̄ is represented by *he*.

Ammonite

bnh (AC 1), *i* > ϵ̄ = *he*
yn (H 1.7, 8), *ay* > ē = Ø (medial position)
bn (TS 1), *ay* > ē = Ø (final position)

Israelite (Samaria)

ymnh (*KAI* 188.3), *i* > ϵ̄ = *he*
yn (*KAI* 185.2), *ay* > ē = Ø (medial position)

Judahite

yqrh (*AI* 24.16), *i* > ϵ̄ = *he*
byt (*KAI* 194.5), *ay* > ē (or *ay*) = *yod* (medial position; see the following discussion)
spry (*KAI* 196.4), *ay* > ē (or *ay*) = *yod* (final position). It is not clear whether the contraction *ay* > ē had taken place in Judahite by the period of these texts (cf. Cross and Freedman 1952: 57; Freedman 1969:

52–53, 55; Parunak 1978: 25, 30; Zevit 1980: chap. 4). In any case there was an orthographic distinction made between the sounds represented by *yod* and *he*.

Moabite, *KAI* 181

yhwh (18), *i* > ε̄ = *he*

bt (23), *ay* > ē = Ø (medial position)

ymy (8), *ay* > ē = *yod* (final position)

These examples show a consistent pattern of distinguishing orthographically between ε̄ and ē.

The data from the inscriptions and the Bible do not prove conclusively the distinction between ē and ε̄, since *historical* considerations may underlie the orthographic difference. The two sounds and their orthographies have different origins. The *yod* used to represent ē in other Canaanite texts and in the Bible is a historical spelling which was established in the orthography while the sound it represented (the diphthong *ay*) still had a consonantal element. It only came to represent a vowel—after the spelling was fixed—when the original consonantal element was lost in the contraction and only the vowel ē remained. In contrast, the *he* is a *mater lectionis*, representing a vowel sound which has no historical or evolutionary relationship to the consonantal phoneme *h* in most places where it is used, as in *'bnh* (= **'ibnε̄́* < **'abnī́* < **'ábni* < **'ábniu*) (see Cross and Freedman 1952: 31 *et passim* for the origin of nonhistorical vowel letters). The generally conservative orthographic practices of the Canaanite scribes, including those who recorded the Hebrew Bible, may have preserved and perpetuated for centuries the distinction between these two historically different spellings, even though there may have been no distinction in pronunciation.

It is possible that by the time of the earliest Ammonite text, the Citadel inscription, there was no longer a distinction between the two sounds. It appears however that there was a distinction at one time, since in the Ammonite inscriptions the sounds are represented in two different ways. The contracted diphthong is consistently unrepresented (i.e., written Ø); ε̄ appears twice in Ammonite (AC 1; AT 1) and is written with *he* in both places. If these represent the same sound, then this complementary system of spelling is based on a historical distinction in pronunciation. At the time when the orthography was established by the Ammonite scribal school, *'bnh* (AT 1) probably was pronounced **'ibnɛ̄*, and the imperative *bnh* (AC 1) probably was pronounced **banɛ̄*. But the contraction of *ay* had been completed by this time, and mpl cstr *bn* (TS 1, 2, 3; AC 6; AT 2) was pronounced **banē*. We cannot be certain whether or how long the pronunciation difference lasted. Yet if ɛ̄ later fell together with ē, removing the phonemic distinction, then the orthographic difference observed in the Ammonite texts can be explained historically.

I have retained the distinction, since the evidence is in favor of the existence of two separate sounds. Other possibilities cannot be ruled out.

Word Division

There is a word divider in line 1 between *b'l* and *'bnh*. There is none between *bn* and *'m[n* in line 2, which constitute a construct chain.

Linguistic Affiliation of the Amman Theater Inscription

The one noun and one verb of this inscription are two of the most common words in Canaanite: *bn* (noun) and *bny* (verb). From the meager evidence provided, there is no reason to believe that the Theater inscription is written in anything but Ammonite, the language which already has been identified in the other inscriptions examined in this study.

CHAPTER FIVE
THE HESHBON OSTRACA

Introduction

The excavations conducted at tell Ḥisbān in Jordan (biblical Ḥešbôn) during the 1960s and 1970s provided additional Ammonite texts to our corpus. In this analysis I have included the only texts worthy of study (for additional fragments, wherein no complete words are preserved, cf. Cross 1975: 19–20). All of the texts were published by F. M. Cross: H 1 (1975: 1–18); H 2 (1976: 145–48); H 3 (1983); H 4 (1973b: 126–31); H 5 (1969b: 223–29); H 6 (1975: 18–19). Inscriptions 1–3 and 6 are Ammonite, both in language and script. Nos. 4 and 5 are Aramaic. They are included here only because of the Ammonite personal names that they preserve. Only the names from these inscriptions will be included in the lists and analyses that follow. All of the dates given for the Heshbon ostraca are those of Cross.

Though the texts do not make up a corpus in any but the loosest sense of the word, I will present them together for the sake of convenience.

Texts and Translations

Heshbon 1

Text:

1. l]mlk . ʾkl 20 + 10 + 5 (?) [
2. wṣʾn 8
3. wlndbʾl bn nʿmʾl m[
4. lz[ ]mʾlt nkʾt 10 + 2 ʾk̊[l
5. l[ ] nkʾt 2 ʾrḥ bt 2 w[
6. lbʿš[ʾ] ksp 20 + 20 ʾš ntn l[
7. yn 20 + 2 wṣʾn 10 lbbt [

8. yn 8 w'kl 6
9. lytb dš' 'kl 20 + 4 (?)
10. ṣ'n 9
11. 'rḥ bt 3

Translation:

1. To] the king: 35 (units of) grain [
2. and 8 small cattle.
3. And to Nadab'il son of Na'īm'il from [
4. To Z[ ] from Elat: 12 (units of) gum; g[rain
5. To [ ] 2 (units of) gum; a two-year-old cow and [
6. To Ba'ša[']: 40 (units of) silver, which he gave to [
7. 22 (units of) wine; and 10 small cattle; cakes [
8. 8 (units of) wine; and 6 (units of) grain.
9. To YTB: hay; 24 (units of) grain;
10. 9 small cattle;
11. a three-year-old cow.

Date: ca. 600

Script: Ammonite

Cross characterizes this text as being "of exceptional interest" (1975: 1). It may be the record of a transaction involving the distribution or delivery of commodities, probably from the royal storehouse. The recipients are the king himself and a number of other individuals who probably were members of the Ammonite aristocracy. The possibility also exists that this is a list of gifts to a temple (Cross 1975: 7–10).

This document makes an important contribution to our knowledge of Ammonite, especially because of the eleven nouns that can be identified in it. Of special value are the words which contribute to an understanding of Ammonite phonology and/or linguistic affinity, e.g., the relative pronoun *'š*, the noun *yn*, and the verb *ntn* (see the discussion of linguistic affiliation, below). For a fuller treatment of the text, cf. Cross 1975: 1–18.

Heshbon 2

Text:

1. t’n [
2. t’n mn[
3. b‘rm [
4. ḥblm [

Translation:

1. figs [
2. figs from N[
3. beasts of burden [
4. ropes [

Date: ca. 575

Script: Ammonite

This inscription contributes three nouns and a preposition to our knowledge of Ammonite. For further discussion cf. Cross 1976: 145–48.

Heshbon 3

Text:

1. lḥ̊š̊[ ]n̊ [
2. ’lrm bn h̊w[ ]l̊ [
3. ‘zr’l bn [
4. ’l‘zr b̊n m̊lk’l [
5. nqr ’l’wr 1
6. ’lndb brq 1
7.]pr̊š bn ḥmšgb 1
8.]’ bn šm̊š’l 1
9. ‘]zr bn šql 1
10.]n bn ‘qb 1
11. ’]l bnny 2
12.]’̊l q[
13.
14.]lb̊ṣrt

Translation:

1. To Ḥeš[b]ōn [

2. 'Ilīram son of HW[ ]L̊ [
3. 'Azar'il son of [
4. 'Il'azar son of Malkī'il [
5. NQR (son of) 'Ilī'ûr: 1
6. 'Ilnadab (son of) Baraq: 1
7.]Paraš son of Ḥamīśagab: 1
8.]' son of Šamšī'il: 1
9. ']ZR son of ŠQL: 1
10.]N son of 'Aqūb: 1
11. ']L Binōnî: 2
12.]ʾL Q[
13.
14.]LB̊ṢRT

Date: ca. 550–525

Script: Ammonite

For detailed analysis of this text, especially with regard to paleography, cf. Cross 1983. For analysis of the personal names, cf. Jackson 1983.

Heshbon 4

Text:

1.]n[
2. skt pd[
3. tmk'l [
4. bny gbl[

Translation:

1.
2. Sukkoth PD[
3. Tamak'il [
4. Byblians [

Date: ca. 525

Script: Aramaic

This inscription is small and quite fragmentary. Line 2 is especially difficult (cf. Shea 1977: 217–20). Because this text is written in Aramaic (script and language), the data contained in it will not be analyzed or included in the lists below, except for the Ammonite personal name *tmk'l*. For further information, cf. Cross 1973b: 126–31.

Heshbon 5

Text:

1. bn l[
2. 'zy'[l
3. bn rp'[
4. bn psmy [
5. nnydn 1 [

Translation:

1. Son of L[
2. 'Uzzî'i[l
3. Son of Rapa'[
4. Son of Psammî [
5. Nanaydan: 1 [

Date: ca. 500

Script: Aramaic

For further analysis, cf. Cross 1969b: 223–29. This text is included for its onomastic information only.

Heshbon 6

Text:

n]tn'l .

Date: 7th century

Script: Ammonite

Cf. Cross 1975: 18–19.

Lexicon

'kl	nm (1.1, 4 [?], 8, 9) food, grain
'rḥ	nf (1.5, 11) cow
'š	rel prn (1.6) which, that
bn	nm(1.3; 3.2, 3, 4, 7, 8, 9, 10; 5.1, 3, 4 = cstr) son

b‘r	nm (2.3 = b‘rm, pl) beast of burden
bt	nf (1.5, 11 = cstr) daughter
dš’	nm (1.9) grass, hay
w-	conj (1.2, 3, 5, 7, 8) and
ḥbl	nm (2.4 = ḥblm, pl) rope
yn	nm (1.7, 8) wine
ksp	nm (1.6) silver, silver piece
l-	prep (1.3, 4, 5, 6bis, 9; 3.1) to, for
lbbt	nf (1.7 = lbbt, fpl) loaf, cake
m-	prep (1.3, 4) from
mlk	nm (1.1) king
nk’t	nf (1.4, 5) a gum or spice
ntn	vb (1.6 = *Qal* pf 3ms) give
ṣ’n	nm (1.2, 7, 10) small cattle
t’n	nm (2.1, 2) fig

Personal Names

’l’wr	(3.5)
’lndb	(3.6)
’l‘zr	(3.4)
’lrm	(3.2)
bnny	(3.11)
b‘š[’	(1.6)
brq	(3.6)
ḥmšgb	(3.7)
ytb	(1.9)
m̊lk’l	(3.4)
ndb’l	(1.3)
nnydn	(5.5)
n‘m’l	(1.3)
nqr	(3.5)
n]tn’l	(6)
‘zy’[l	(5.2)
‘zr’l	(3.3)
‘qb	(3.10)
psmy	(5.4)
pr̊š	(3.7)
rp’	(5.3)

šm̊š’l	(3.8)
šql	(3.9)
tmk’l	(4.3)

Place Names

’lt	(1.4)
ḥ̊š̊[b]n̊	(3.1)

Morphology

1. *Nouns*

a) Attested forms:

’kl (1.1, 4 [?], 8, 9)	ms
’rḥ (1.5, 11)	fs
bn (1.3; 3.2, 3, 4, 7, 8, 9, 10; 5.1, 3, 4)	ms cstr
b‘rm (2.3)	mpl
bt (1.5, 11)	fs cstr
dš’ (1.9)	ms
ḥblm (2.4)	mpl
yn (1.7, 8)	ms
ksp (1.6)	ms
lbbt (1.7)	fpl
mlk (1.1)	ms
nk’t (1.4, 5)	fs
ṣ’n (1.2, 7, 10)	ms
t’n (2.1)	ms

b) Inflections:

ms:	’kl	-Ø
	dš’	-Ø
	yn	-Ø
	ksp	-Ø
	mlk	-Ø
	ṣ’n	-Ø
	t’n	-Ø
ms cstr:	bn	-Ø
mpl:	b‘rm	-m (-īm)
	ḥblm	-m (-īm)

fs:	’rḥ	-∅
	nk’t	-t (-at)
fs cstr:	bt	-t (-at)
fpl:	lbbt	-t (-ōt)

2. *Verb*

ntn (1.6) *Qal* pf 3ms - - -

3. *Prepositions*

l- (1.3, 4, 5, 6bis, 9; 3.1)
m- (1.3, 4)

4. *Conjunction*

w- (1.2, 3, 5, 7, 8)

5. *Relative Pronoun*

’š (1.6)

Summary

a) *Nouns*: The Heshbon ostraca are rich in nouns, allowing us to identify a paradigm of all of the nominal inflections but the mpl cstr and the fpl cstr forms: ms (-∅), ms cstr (-∅), mpl (*-īm*), fs (-∅), fs (*-at*), fs cstr (*-at*), and fpl (*-ōt*). These inflections are identical to those of the Tell Siran inscription and the Amman Citadel inscription, as far as they are attested.

b) *Verb*, *prepositions*, and *conjunction*: The only verb of the Heshbon collection is a *Qal* perfect, one of only two perfect verbs found in all of Ammonite (cf. *ndr*, AS 49). It is morphologically and orthographically identical to the *Qal* perfect of Hebrew. The prepositions and conjunction show no divergences from the patterns known from other Canaanite dialects.

Phonology and Orthography

There is no evidence in the Heshbon ostraca for any orthographic practices which differ from those demonstrated in the other Ammonite inscriptions of the same period. The orthography of *yn* (1.7, 8) demonstrates that the contraction *ay* > *ē* had taken place by this period and that the resulting vowel was not represented orthographically in internal position (cf. *‘lk*, AC 2; contrast the uncontracted diphthong *aw* in *ywmt*, TS 7). The *'alep* in *ṣ'n* (1.2, 7, 10) may be a historical spelling. According to Harris (1939: 42), it lost its consonantal value in this position as early as the Amarna period, as it was assimilated into the preceding vowel in the doubly closed syllable created by the loss of the case ending; i.e., **ṣa'nu* > **ṣa'n* > **ṣān* > **ṣōn* (Bergsträsser 1918: 89; cf. Bauer and Leander 1922: #25*b*). This is hardly conclusive, however, and it is possible that the persistence of the grapheme *'alep* may indicate the retention of an internal glottal stop.

Matres lectionis in the ostraca are found only in names.

'l'wr (3.5): **'Ilī'ûr*, with the *waw* representing medial *ū*.

bnny (3.11): The final *yod* is a *mater lectionis* for *ī*.

'zy'[l (5.2): **'Uzzī'i[l* (cf. Cross 1969b: 228); the *yod* represents a medial *ī*. Cf. the discussion of AS 40 and references there.

psmy (5.4): An Egyptian name with the final *ī* represented by *yod* (Cross 1969b: 228).

Word Division

The Heshbon ostraca preserve only two word dividers (1.1; 6). Separation of words by the addition of extra space is not consistent.

Linguistic Affiliation of the Heshbon Ostraca

The ostraca from Heshbon studied here are written in Ammonite. The lexicon and morphology show its place among the other Canaanite languages.

Lexicon

Of the identifiable nouns and the one identifiable verb in the ostraca from Heshbon, all but one are attested in the Hebrew Bible, though Ammonite *t'n* has a different gender than its Hebrew counterpart. The exception is *'rḥ* (1.5, 11). Cross (1975: 5) presents a convincing argument for translating this as "cow." Cognates are found in Ugaritic (*arḫ*, Gordon 1965: 365), Akkadian (*arḫu*, *CAD* A, part 2: 263), and Sinaitic (*'rḫt*, texts no. 353, 365b,

Albright 1966: 22, 27). It is not attested elsewhere in Canaanite, nor in Aramaic. The Biblical Hebrew cognate of *t'n* (2.1) is *tĕ'ēnâ*, which, unlike our Ammonite example, is a feminine noun. Yet Biblical Hebrew *tĕ'ēnâ* regularly takes the mpl endings (e.g., *tĕ'ēnê* and *tĕ'ēnîm*, both from Jer 24:2). Dialectal preference for a certain gender (or a certain gender-related inflectional ending) as opposed to another has been noted already in Ammonite: **gannat* (TS 4, contrasting to the regular BH *gan*), **yawmōt* (TS 7, contrasting to the regular BH *yāmîm*), **šanōt* (TS 7, contrasting to the regular BH *šānîm*, though the BH singular is *šānâ*), and **mabō'ōt* (AC 1, contrasting to BH mpl cstr *mĕbô'ê*). The Biblical Hebrew exceptions to what I have called "regular BH," some of which are identical to the Ammonite forms, have been noted in the discussions of the individual forms throughout this study.

The form of "to give," *ntn* (1.6), is instructive. This form is found in Judahite (*KAI* 194.11; and throughout Biblical Hebrew, *BDB*: 678–82) and Moabite (*kmšntn*, Herr 1978: 156; *bʿlntn*, Herr 1978: 158) and contrasts with Phoenician *ytn* (*KAI* 14.18; cf. Harris 1939: 37).

The most notable lexical item in the Heshbon materials is the relative pronoun *'š* (1.6). This is the regular (although not the only) relative pronoun of Phoenician in all dialects but 10th-century Byblian (*'rn . zpʿl*, *KAI* 1.1; *qr . zbny*, *KAI* 7.1; but *'š pʿltn*, *KAI* 10.2, 5th–4th century; etc.; cf. Harris 1936: 54–55; *PPG*²: #121). It contrasts with Hebrew *'šr* (*KAI* 192.6; Biblical Hebrew *'ăšer*) and Moabite *'šr* (*KAI* 181.29). Mishnaic Hebrew *še-* (Segal 1927: 204–6) is related, as are Biblical Hebrew *še-* (*BDB*: 979–80) and *ša-*, found often in the Bible in passages of supposedly North Israelite origin (e.g., *ʿad šaqqamtî dĕbôrâ šaqqamtî 'ēm bĕyiśrā'ēl*, Judg 5:7). The relative pronoun *š-* has also been found in an Ammonite seal; cf. the discussion of AS 49, chap. 7.

There can be no doubt from the lexical evidence that the Ammonite of the Heshbon ostraca belongs to the Canaanite family. Every attested lexical item but one (*'rḥ*, 1.5, 11) has cognates in other Iron Age Canaanite languages (and *arḫ* is found in Bronze Age Canaanite, Gordon 1965: 365). The diagnostic words *ntn* and *'š* (both 1.6) and their respective isoglosses—*ntn* pointing toward Hebrew and Moabite (and away from Phoenician), and *'š* pointing toward Phoenician (and away from Hebrew and Moabite)—demonstrate that the Ammonites had their own language with its special features. It was definitely distinguishable from its sister tongues. This distinction is borne out further by the unique gender of some of the Ammonite nouns, as noted above.

Morphology

The morphology of the nouns found in the Heshbon corpus is identical to that observed in the other Ammonite epigraphs examined in this study: ms (-Ø), ms cstr (-Ø), mpl (*-īm*), mpl cstr (*-ē*), fs (-Ø), fs (*-at*), fs cstr (*-at*), fpl (*-ōt*). This paradigm is similar to that of Phoenician (cf. Harris 1936: 58–60). Judahite differs from Ammonite in the use of the fs termination *-â*; Moabite differs in the use of the mpl termination *-īn*.

CHAPTER SIX
THE NIMRUD OSTRACON

Introduction

In 1957 an ostracon discovered at Nineveh was published by J. B. Segal under the title "An Aramaic Ostracon from Nimrud" (1957: 139–45). Shortly thereafter W. F. Albright discussed the text and identified it as the product of exiles from (North) Israel in the early years of the Israelite diaspora (1958: 35–36). The text is written on both sides of the ostracon in three columns, two on one side and one on the other, in a total of fifteen lines. According to Naveh (1980: 163), the writing is the product of two hands. The text itself consists almost entirely of names.

Because of the provenience of the sherd and the script preserved on it, which is of the Aramaic family, the ostracon has received little attention from scholars dealing in Canaanite epigraphs, in spite of the fact that Canaanite *bn* is used exclusively, rather than Aramaic *br*. Recently, however, Joseph Naveh published a reexamination of it (1980: 163–71) in which he identified the language of the inscription as Ammonite, based on the personal names listed. Naveh's assessment is undoubtedly correct. The names listed on the ostracon fit the pattern of Ammonite names better than that of any of the other languages. Of the twenty names preserved, seven are found in other Ammonite inscriptions: *'lyš'*, *byd'l*, *ḥnn'l*, *m]k'l* (cf. *mkm'l*, AS 35), *mnḥm*, *ndb'l*, and *šb'l*. Moreover, of those names which are not attested elsewhere in Ammonite, six contain verbal elements found in other Ammonite names: *'yndb*, *'lnr*, *'ltmk*, *blntn*, *ḥnn*, and *'z'*. Perhaps the most telling datum for identifying the names on the list as Ammonite is the use of the theophoric element *'l*. The name *'l* is found in almost half of the Ammonite names attested (see the complete list of names in chap. 8 and Jackson 1983), a far greater percentage than in any other Northwest-Semitic language. Eleven of the twenty names on the Nimrud ostracon contain *’l*.

In this study I will not provide anything more than minimal comment on the inscription. Naveh has treated the script (1970a: 14, fig. 2, lines 3 and 4), and Albright (1958: 33–36) and Naveh (1980: 163–71) have treated the names, as I have elsewhere (Jackson 1983), obviating the need for detailed discussion here.

Text

1. b]n ‘n’l .
2. ḥ̊nn’l bn ‘n’l
3. mnḥm . bn byd’l
4. šb’l . bn ‘z’
5. ḥnn’l . bn ḥz’l .
6. gn’ . bn mnḥm .
7. ’lnr . bn m<n>ḥm
8. ’lnr . bn [ ]’l
9. . zkr’l . bn ṣnr
10. ndb’l . bn ḥnn .
11. mnḥm . bn ’lyš‘
12. ’lnr . bn [m]k’l .
13. ’yndb . bn ḥgy .
14. ’ltmk . kbs
15. ‘kbr . blntn

Translation

1. . . . so]n of ‘Ana’il
2. Ḥanan’il son of ‘Ana’il
3. Mĕnaḥḥim son of Bayad’il
4. ŠB’L son of ‘Uzza’
5. Ḥanan’il son of Ḥaza’il
6. GN’ son of Mĕnaḥḥim
7. ’Ilīnur son of Mĕnaḥḥim
8. ’Ilīnur son of [ ]’il
9. Zakar’il son of Ṣinnōr
10. Nadab’il son of Ḥanūn
11. Mĕnaḥḥim son of ’Ilyaša‘
12. ’Ilīnur son of [Mī]ka’il
13. ’Aynadab son of Ḥaggî

14. ’Iltamak (the) launderer
15. ‘Akbor (son of) Belnatan

Philological Comments

The reading of the text is essentially that of Naveh (1980: 164). The transliterations of the names are those proposed in Jackson 1983.

Line 4

šb’l: The vocalization of this name is uncertain. M. P. O’Connor reads it as an imperative name, “Turn/Return, O ’Il” (personal communication).

Line 7

m<n>ḥm: The emendation has been proposed by Albright (1958: 33) and Naveh (1980: 164). It is undoubtedly correct. *mnḥm* is the most common name in the Ammonite onomasticon.

Line 11

’lyšʿ: Cf. the discussion of this name in chap. 7 under AS 58.

Line 12

m]k’l: Albright’s proposed reading of the obscure first letter yields **mīka’il*. Compare the biform of this name preserved in AS 35, *mkm’l* = **mīkamō’il*, and the syntactically similar transliteration from Akkadian, *mng’nrt* = **mannu-kī-inurta* in AS 36.

Line 14

kbs: Albright interpreted this word as an Aramaic spelling of the Hebrew word *kebeś* (BH), “lamb” (1958: 34, n. 13). I can find little justification for assuming either Aramaic influence or some kind of s/ś interchange in operation here. Naveh’s proposed “washer, launderer, fuller,” from the root *kbs*, “to wash,” is better (1980: 170). The question that remains is whether the word is a name, the patronymic of *’ltmk*, or whether it is *’ltmk*’s professional identification, as Naveh reads it. Naveh points to the absence of *bn* as evidence that the word is not the patronymic. Yet Ammonite preserves other examples of patronymic references not preceded by *bn*: *nqr 'l'wr*, "NQR (son of) 'Ilī'ûr" (H 3.5); *'lndb brq*, "'Ilnadab (son of) Baraq" (H 3.6); *yš' 'd'l*, "Yaša' (son of) 'Adī'il" (AS 56); and *'kbr blntn*, "'Akbor (son of) Belnatan" (NO 15). Since the following line, *'kbr blntn*, cited above, also omits the *bn*, it is not unreasonable to read *kbs* as a name. The absence of the definite article is surprising before an occupational designation, if that is what it is. Naveh's reference to the lack of the article in the construct chain *'bd mlk* (AS 17) (1980: 170) is not relevant here.

Line 15

blntn: For the absence of *bn*, cf. the discussion of line 14, above. Naveh proposes "*bl ntn*—a dissimilation of *bn ntn*" (1980: 164, n. 5). This seems to be unnecessary. The name means "Bēl (<Akkadian<West-Semitic *ba'al*) has given." The Ammonite onomasticon preserves several names with elements not indigenous to Canaanite, e.g., *'w'* (AS 47), *b'š[* (H 1.6), *mng'nrt* (AS 36), *nnydn* (H 5.5), *'nmwt* (AS 57), *psmy* (H 5.4), etc.

Lexicon

bn nm (1, 2, 3, 4, 5, 6, 7, 8, 9, 10, 11, 12, 13 = cstr) son
kbs vb (14 = *Qal* act pcp ms) wash, launder

Personal Names

'yndb	(13)
'lyš'	(11)
'lnr	(7, 8, 12)
'ltmk	(14)
byd'l	(3)
blntn	(15)
gn'	(6)
zkr'l	(9)
ḥgy	(13)
ḥz'l	(5)

ḥnn	(10)
ḥnn'l	(2, 5)
m]k'l	(12)
mnḥm	(3, 6, 7, 11)
ndb'l	(10)
ʿz'	(4)
ʿkbr	(15)
ʿn'l	(1, 2)
ṣnr	(9)
šb'l	(4)

Morphology

The noun and verb preserved in the Nimrud ostracon conform to the patterns observed elsewhere in Ammonite.

Phonology and Orthography

The words found in the Nimrud ostracon preserve no internal vowel letters; e.g., internal ī in *'lnr* = **'ilīnur* (7, 8, 12) is not represented orthographically (for which cf. the discussion of AS 40, chap. 7). Final vowel letters indicate hypocoristic endings: *'alep* in *gn'* (6) and *ʿz'* (4), and *yod* in *ḥgy* (13). The *yod* in *'yndb* (13) is that of an uncontracted diphthong. Albright's comments on this name are informative (1958: 34, n. 12). Compare Biblical Hebrew *'îkābôd* (1 Sam 4:21).

Word Division

The Nimrud ostracon is essentially consistent in the use of word dividers, which separate the initial personal names from *bn* that follows. The construct chains *bn* PN are not interrupted by dividers.

Linguistic Affiliation of the Nimrud Ostracon

For discussion concerning the identification of the Nimrud ostracon as Ammonite, cf. the comments above and Naveh 1980: 163–65.

CHAPTER SEVEN
AMMONITE SEALS

Introduction

In addition to the larger texts, Ammonite seals provide significant information for the study of that language. Though they contribute little to the study of morphology, they do contain information which is of value in observing the development of the Ammonite spelling system, particularly in the use of vowel letters in names.

The following list contains all of the Ammonite seals of which I am aware. Translation and discussion will be limited to those that contain features which contribute positively to the analysis of Ammonite linguistic and orthographic traits. Thus words which contain *matres lectionis* will be discussed, while words which do not will receive mention only insofar as they provide a point of contrast to the more fully written forms. The seals are numbered roughly in chronological order, preceded by AS (= Ammonite Seal). Reference to the most convenient sources is supplied for each entry. The dates proposed are those suggested in the sources that follow immediately after the dates. Bibliographical information and paleographic analysis are not presented here but can be found in the sources cited.

This study is not intended to be a thorough analysis of any of the seals; rather its goal is to support the discussions of the larger texts already presented by isolating features of morphological and orthographic interest. For analysis of the personal names contained in the seals, together with complete transliteration, translation, and reference to cognates, cf. Jackson 1983.

With regard to the dating of the seals, most of which is based on paleographic grounds, it should be pointed out by way of caution that the study of Canaanite script types is in its infancy. Some of the dates suggested for the seals in the sources cited, primarily Herr, may not survive future research and future discovery.

The Seals

AS 1 (late 8th century; Herr 1978: 66; Vattioni 1969: no. 166)

l̊mn̊ḥ̊m // b//n ym̊n

AS 2 (late 8th century; Herr 1978: 72; Vattioni 1969: no. 88)

ʿšn'l

Classified by Herr as "probable Ammonite" (1978: 72).

AS 3 (late 8th–early 7th century; Herr 1978: 66; Vattioni 1971: no. 264)

lmnḥm // bn tnḥm

AS 4 (late 8th–early 7th century; Herr 1978: 66)

lʿms'l

AS 5 (late 8th–mid-7th century; Herr 1978: 68)

l'lš//mʿ

AS 6 (ca. 700; Herr 1978: 59)

lbyd'l ʿbd pd'l

The first name, *byd'l*, is vocalized *bĕyōd'ēl* by Cross (1974: 494). He prefers this rendering rather than the alternative *bĕyad'ēl* on the assumption that the Phoenician shift, *á* > ō, was operative in Ammonite. This assumption he bases on the fact that there are "many" Ammonite-Phoenician isoglosses. There is not enough evidence at this point to verify whether the Phoenician shift can be assumed for Ammonite, but it is possible.

AS 7 (ca. 700; Avigad 1977a: 64–65)

obv. lbd'l b/ /n] ndb'l
rev. lbd'l / / bn ndb'l

AS 8 (early 7th century; Herr 1978: 65)

lḥṭš bn / / . . .

AS 9 (early 7th century; Herr 1978: 67)

lšm'l b/ /n plṭw

Cognates of the name *plṭw* are attested in Biblical Hebrew (1 Chr 2:47), Ugaritic (Gröndahl 1967: 173), and elsewhere in West Semitic texts (Jackson 1983). The final *waw* probably is a hypocoristic ending; the most likely vocalization is *ū*.

AS 10 (early 7th century; Herr 1978: 67)

ltmk[ ]/ / bn / / mqnmlk

AS 11 (early 7th century; Herr 1978: 69)

l'lndb bn 'lydn

The second name can be either **'ilîdan*, "My God is judge" or "'Il is judge," or **'ilyadīn*, "My God shall judge" or "'Il shall judge." There is no way to tell from the orthography. The latter vocalization is supported by Akkadian transcriptions of the name from Babylonian documents of the 5th century: [1]*DINGIR.MEŠ.-ya-a-di-ni* and [1]*DINGIR.MEŠ.ya-a-di-in* (Coogan 1976: 13).

AS 12 (700–650; Herr 1978: 63; Vattioni 1969: no. 201)

lndb'l / / bn 'ms'l

AS 13 (first half of the 7th century?; Herr 1978: 72)

lšm'

"Probable Ammonite" (Herr 1978: 73), having paleographic similarities with Aramaic.

AS 14 (early to mid-7th century; Herr 1978: 65; Vattioni 1971: no. 262)

'l' // bn ḥṭš

AS 15 (early to mid-7th century; Herr 1978: 67; Vattioni 1969: no. 165)

l̊šb'l

AS 16 (700–650; Bordreuil and Lemaire 1976: 59–60)

ltmk'l // bn plṭy

The distinguishing orthographic feature of this seal is the hypocoristic ending ī, represented by a *mater lectionis, yod.*

AS 17 (700–650; Avigad 1977a: 63–64)

lmnḥm bn smk // ʿbd mlk

AS 18 (ca. 675–650; Herr 1978: 59; Vattioni 1969: no. 164)

l'dnnr . ʿ//bd ʿmndb

AS 19 (ca. 675–650; Herr 1978: 59; Vattioni 1969: no. 98)

l'dnplṭ // ʿbd ʿmndb

AS 20 (675–650; Herr 1978: 70)

l'lyʿm

This name is attested in the Bible, *'ĕlîʿām* (2 Sam 11:3; 2 Sam 23:34), and means "My God is kinsman" or "'Il is kinsman." It is also found in Punic (*'lʿm, CIS* 147.6) and in pre-Islamic Arabic (Harding 1971: 68). Note the internal *mater lectionis yod*; cf. AS 40, 58.

AS 21 (7th century; Herr 1978: 68)

lmrʿ

AS 22 (7th century; Herr 1978: 70)

l'ltmk b/ /n 'ms'l

AS 23 (7th century; Herr 1978: 73)

lšm'

"Possible Ammonite seal" (Herr 1978: 73).

AS 24 (7th century; Bordreuil and Lemaire 1976: 58–59)

ltmk'l

AS 25 (7th century; Bordreuil and Lemaire 1976: 59)

lndb'l / / bn / / tmk'

The hypocoristic ending *'alep* of *tmk'* likely represents an *a* vowel.

AS 26 (7th century; Bordreuil and Lemaire 1976: 60)

lplṭ

AS 27 (7th century; Bordreuil and Lemaire 1976: 60–61)

obv. l'lšm' / / bn b'r'
rev. l'lšm'

The name *b'r'* contains the hypocoristic termination *'alep*, probably representing the vowel sound *a*.

AS 28 (7th century; Bordreuil and Lemaire 1976: 61)

lmnḥm b/ /n mgr'l

AS 29 (7th century; Bordreuil and Lemaire 1976: 61–62)

l'lntn / / bn ytyr

The name *ytyr* is most difficult. The medial *yod* is most likely consonantal.

AS 30 (Bordreuil and Lemaire 1976: 62–63)

lmnr

AS 31 (7th century; Bordreuil and Lemaire 1976: 63)

'bgdhẘ//zḥṭykl

This seal contributes to our knowledge of Ammonite only as it demonstrates the order of the first twelve letters of the Canaanite alphabet as perceived by the scribes of Ammon.

AS 32 (7th century; Puech 1976: 60–61)

l'l'z b//n mnḥm

The name *'l'z*, **'ilī'uz*, contains no orthographic representation for the internal 1st person possessive pronoun.

AS 33 (7th century; Avigad 1978: 68)

l'lš//m'

AS 34 (Cross 1983)

l'l'mt bn 'l'wr

The name *'l'wr*, **'ilī'ûr*, is attested in Ammonite also in H 3.5. The 1st person possessive pronoun is not represented in the orthography. However, the long vowel of the element *'ūr*, "light," is represented by *waw*. This is a *mater lectionis*.

AS 35 (7th century; Avigad 1977b: 110)

lmk//m'l

The name *mkm'l* is a biform of the name *mk'l*, "Who is like 'Il," which is found in Ammonite in NO 12.

AS 36 (mid-7th century; Herr 1978: 62; Vattioni 1969: no. 225)

ḥtm . mng'nr//t brk lmlkm

AS 37 (mid-7th century; Herr 1978: 62; Vattioni 1971: no. 263)

lndb'l // bn 'l'zr

AS 38 (mid-7th century; Herr 1978: 68–69; Vattioni 1969: no. 133)

obv. l'lybr // bn mnḥm
rev. l'lybr

The first name probably should be vocalized **'ilîbar*, "My God is purity/pure" or "'Il is purity/pure" (cf. BH *bōr*, "cleanliness, pureness" and *bar*, "pure, clean"). The internal *mater lectionis yod* is also found elsewhere in Ammonite names.

AS 39 (mid-7th century; Herr 1978: 71)

l'bd

AS 40 (650–625; Herr 1978: 60; Vattioni 1969: no. 103)

l'byḥy // bt // ynḥm

The first *yod* in *'byḥy*, **'abîḥay*, is an internal *mater lectionis* (cf. Stamm 1967: 315–16). Almost all of the biblical names which have *'b* or *'ḥ* as the first element have ī appended to that element, represented by *yod*, before the second element of the name (*BDB*: 3–5, 26–27; Noth 1928: 234–36). The ī is of course not represented orthographically in Phoenician names of the same type (e.g., *'ḥrm*, *KAI* 1.1; *'bb'l*, *KAI* 5.1; cf. Benz 1972: 54–55, 61, 224), but it certainly was pronounced (Donner and Röllig 1962–64 II: 3, 8; Benz 1972: 211). This is borne out in Akkadian transcriptions of Canaanite names: [1]*a-bi-ba-'-al*, Annals of Ašurbanipal II.82 (Streck 1916: 18, 19; cf. Bauer 1933: 4), and [1]*a-bi-mil-ki*, Annals of Ašurbanipal II.84 (Streck 1916: 20, 21). The name *'byḥy* is found also in Palmyrene Aramaic inscriptions (Stark 1971: 1), spelled exactly as the AS 40 example. The ī generally is considered to be the 1st person possessive pronoun (Benz 1972: 232; contra Noth 1928: 33, 68). It is unlikely that the medial *yod* in *'byḥy* is the preformative of an imperfect verb. There are no attested names in Biblical Hebrew (Noth 1928: 67) or epigraphic Canaanite (Benz 1972: 208–10;

Herr 1978: 208) which consist of either *'b* or *'ḥ* followed by a verb in the imperfect. Therefore (and lacking any evidence for a verbal root *yḥy*) it is best to read the *yod* as an internal *mater lectionis*. Note in contrast the defective spelling of *'bndb* in AS 49, but cf. the similar *matres lectionis* in *'lybr* (AS 38), *'ly'm* (AS 20), *'zy'[l* (H 5.2; Cross 1969b: 228), and possibly *'lyš'* (AS 46, 54, 58). The final *yod* in *'byḥy* is consonantal and represents the diphthong *ay*, which remained uncontracted in this word as in Phoenician; cf. *bḥym*, *KAI* 14.12; 53:1.

AS 41 (mid- to late 7th century; Herr 1978: 65; Vattioni 1969: no. 159)

lbqš b//n ndb'l

AS 42 (Bordreuil and Lemaire 1976: 62)

l'l//mšl

AS 43 (650–600; Herr 1978: 74; Vattioni 1969: no. 135)

pd'l

"Possible Ammonite seal" (Herr 1978: 73).

AS 44 (late 7th century; Herr 1978: 60; Vattioni 1969: no. 115)

l'l'mṣ // bn 'lš'

For the orthography of *'lš'*, cf. the discussion of AS 58.

AS 45 (late 7th century; Herr 1978: 61; Vattioni 1971: no. 259)

l'mr'l // bn ynḥm

AS 46 (late 7th century; Herr 1978: 64; Vattioni 1969: no. 41)

lš'l b//n 'lyš'

Note the possible *mater lectionis yod* in *'lyš'*; cf. AS 44, 54, and the discussion of AS 58.

AS 47 (late 7th century; Herr 1978: 64; Vattioni 1969: no. 194)

l'w' b//n mr'l

AS 48 (late 7th century; Herr 1978: 70)

yš''l

AS 49 (late 7th century; Herr 1978: 71)

. . . bn] // 'bndb šnd//r l'št bṣdn // tbrkh

PN son of] 'Abīnadab. (This is) what he vowed to 'Aš<tar>t in Sidon. May she bless him.

If this is established to be Ammonite, it will be the most important seal of the entire corpus, as it provides valuable lexical and morphological data. Its provenience is unknown.

The name 'Abīnadab is otherwise unattested in Ammonite, but it occurs several times in the Hebrew Bible (*'ăbînādāb*, 1 Sam 7:1; 1 Sam 16:8; etc.); it is not found in Phoenician (cf. Benz 1972: 54). For the orthography cf. *'byḥy* in AS 40. The *ndb* element is quite common in Ammonite names, particularly in *'mndb*, "'Ammīnadab" (TS 1, 2; AS 18, 19; cf. [1]*am-mi-na-ad-bi*, the Ammonite king mentioned in the report of Ašurbanipal's first campaign through Syria–Palestine and Egypt, Annals, Cylinder C, I.34; Streck 1916: 140); cf. also *'lndb* (AS 11) and *ndb'l* (AS 12, 37, 41). Avigad (1966: 248) reads *'št* as an abbreviation for *'štrt*, the goddess 'Aštart. Since this shortened spelling occurs only in one other place in the hundreds of West Semitic inscriptions that contain this name (*bd'št*, *CIS* 3568.5/6, Punic), it is perhaps more reasonable to interpret it as the result of a haplography (cf. Benz 1972: 200). However, abbreviated divine names do exist in Phoenician; e.g., *mlqrt*. For the grammar and semantics of *tbrkh*, cf. O'Connor 1977: 5–11.

When he first published the seal, Avigad (1966: 247–51) identified the text as Phoenician, presumably on the basis of its vocabulary (including the names 'Aštart and Sidon) and the dedication and blessing formulas which are so common in Phoenician and Punic inscriptions (O'Connor 1977: 5–11; cf. *KAI* 84; 88; etc.). More recently however, Cross has called it Ammonite (Herr 1978:

71, 77), and Herr's paleographic analysis of the script has led him to conclude likewise: "Certainly the forms are perfect for that tradition during the late 7th century" (1978: 71).

The language of the text clearly is not Phoenician. This inscription has the relative pronoun *š*-, which was not used in Phoenician, in which the regular relative pronoun was *'š* (Harris 1936: 54–55; *PPG*^{2}: #121–22). In Northwest Semitic only Punic (and then only "vulgär und spätpunisch," *PPG*^{2}: #121–22), Israelite (Judg 5:7bis), and Mishnaic Hebrew (Segal 1927: 204–6) have a relative pronoun *š*-.

The 3ms object suffix *-h* on *tbrkh* is also instructive and also demonstrates that the text is not Phoenician. Tyrian-Sidonian Phoenician had two 3ms suffixes, -∅ and *-y*. The former, vocalized **-ō*, is found attached to verbs and nouns which end in consonants. The suffix *-y* is also found on both verbs and nouns but is used only on those which end in vowel sounds; it is vocalized **-yu* (Krahmalkov 1974; cf. Harris 1936: 47–48; *PPG*^{2}: #112). Over most of the history of the Byblian dialect, there was no orthographic difference between the 3ms suffix following consonants and that which followed vowels. The earliest Byblian inscription (*KAI* 1) uses *-h* in both situations (e.g., *mlkh*, "his rule," line 2; *'bh*, "his father," line 1). Later inscriptions use *-w* in all positions (e.g., *zr'w*, "his posterity," *KAI* 10.15; *ymw*, "his days," *KAI* 10.9; *tḥww*, "may she give him life," *KAI* 10.9). The latest attested inscription from Byblos (*KAI* 12), which dates to the 1st century A.D., represents the 3ms suffix following vowels with *-w* (*yḥww*, line 4) and following consonants with -∅ (*ybrk*, line 4). This is closer to, but not identical with, the system used in Tyrian-Sidonian Phoenician.

In both of these dialects it should be noted that there was no orthographic distinction between the 3ms possessive suffix—attached to nouns—and the 3ms object suffix—attached to verbs. The distinction, where one existed, was between the forms attached to words ending in vowels and those ending in consonants. Furthermore, in Phoenician there was no connecting vowel used between imperfect verbs and their suffixes (Krahmalkov 1974: 42). Thus *ybrk* is vocalized **yebarrekō*, "may he bless him," *KAI* 38.2; 41.6; etc. This contrasts with Hebrew, which used a connecting vowel before the suffix on all imperfect verbs except those which already ended in vowels: *$\bar{e}$ + *$h\bar{u}$ = *-$\bar{e}h\bar{u}$. Thus Biblical Hebrew *yĕbārĕkēhû* (Gen 14:19) contrasts with Phoenician **yebarrekō*, cited above.

Aramaic, like Phoenician, has two 3ms suffixes, -*h* and -*hy*. Their use is determined by whether they are attached to consonants (-*h* = *-*ēh*) or vowels (-*hy* = *-*hî*). There was no distinction between those used with nouns and those used with verbs (Rosenthal 1974: #174; Segert 1975: 168).

Moabite uses -*h* to represent the 3ms suffix in all positions. Its vocalization in various environments is a matter of much controversy, but most scholars, following Cross and Freedman (1954: 35–44), reconstruct it on the analogy of Aramaic rather than Hebrew or Phoenician, i.e., *-*ēh* for both the possessive and the object suffixes. However, since the orthography -*h* is extremely ambiguous in this case, there is no way to rule out other possible vocalizations for the Moabite 3ms suffixes, including *-*ōh* for both possessive and object suffix (on the analogy of Phoenician), *-*ōh* possessive and *-*ēhū* object (on the analogy of Hebrew—with the final *ū* not represented orthographically), or something else unique to Moabite.

Judahite appears to fit the pattern known from Biblical Hebrew with regard to the 3ms suffixes following vowel sounds, e.g., *wyʿlhw*, **wayaʿalēhû*, "and they brought him up," *KAI* 194.7. Attached to words ending in consonants, the Judahite 3ms suffix is -*h* (e.g., *ʿbdh*, *KAI* 200.2).

As no other 3ms suffixes have been found in Ammonite, the -*h* from AS 49 under discussion here is unique. There is no way at the present time to determine how it should be vocalized. On the analogy of object suffixes in other Canaanite dialects we might expect something like either *-*ōh* (with Phoenician), *-*ēhū* (with Hebrew), or *-*ōh*/*-*ēhū*/*-*ēh* (with Moabite).

On the paleographical evidence, it appears that the inscription should be classified as Ammonite. If this is true, then we can identify the Ammonite 3ms object suffix as -*h*.

The relative pronoun presents somewhat of a problem with regard to evidence already presented from a different Ammonite source. In H 4.6, which dates from 600, almost contemporaneous with our seal, we have a relative pronoun *ʾš*. Since the readings of both the Heshbon *ʾš* and the *š*- in AS 49 are quite sure, we must posit one of the following conditions to explain the presence of two relative pronouns in this language:

1. Ammonite used both forms—either interchangeably or in complementary distribution with each other depending on criteria which we cannot identify at this time.

2. The *'alep* was inadvertently omitted in AS 49.

3. The text was written in a language other than Ammonite but was incised by an Ammonite scribe. If this is so, the language in question would have to possess both the relative pronoun *š-* and the 3ms object suffix *-h*, as does AS 49. Byblian (*z-* and *-Ø/-w*), Judahite (*'šr* and *-hw*), Moabite (*'šr* and *-h*), and Tyrian-Sidonian Phoenician (*'š* and *-Ø/-y*) can be ruled out. But it is possible that Israelite possessed the combination of *š-* and *-h*. The Israelite inscriptions are mute with regard both to the relative pronoun and the 3ms suffix, but biblical passages which are attributed to the Northern Hebrew dialect exhibit the use of *š-* as the relative pronoun (e.g., Judg 5:7bis). Mishnaic Hebrew, which may belong to the same dialectal stratum of Hebrew as Israelite, has *še-* as its regular relative pronoun (Segal 1927: 204–6). On the basis of the limited information which we possess, it is not impossible to assign the language of AS 49 to Israelite, if it is not Ammonite.

I will classify this seal as Ammonite—though with some reservation—based on the paleography and the linguistic plausibility. Perhaps new information discovered in the future will enable us to classify inscriptions of this sort with greater accuracy.

AS 50 (late 7th century; Herr 1978: 74; Vattioni 1969: no. 217)

l'bd' n//'r 'lrm

"Possible Ammonite seal" (Herr 1978: 74). The first name, *'*abda'*, contains the hypocoristic ending *'alep*.

AS 51 (slightly before 600; Herr 1978: 61; Vattioni 1969: no. 59)

l'lšgb // bt 'lšm'

AS 52 (ca. 600; Herr 1978: 63; Vattioni 1969: no. 157)

l'lyh . '//mt . ḥnn'l

The name *ʿlyh* is otherwise unattested in the Canaanite onomasticon (Benz 1972: 378; Herr 1978: 208; Noth 1928: 253). The *ʿl* element may be a derivative of the root *ʿly*, meaning "high, exalted" (Noth 1928: 146), as in the possibly related biblical name *ʿēlî* (1 Sam 1:3, etc.). The *yod* is most probably a consonant and the *he* a *mater lectionis* for *ā*. Cognates of *ʿlyh* are attested widely in pre-Islamic Arabian languages (Jackson 1983: s.v. *ʿlyh*). Cross suggests that it is a *qutayyilat* diminutive (personal communication).

AS 53 (ca. 600; Herr 1978: 69; Vattioni 1969: no. 221)

lbṭš // nʿr brk//ʾl

AS 54 (ca. 600; Herr 1978: 70; Vattioni 1969: no. 117)

lʾly//šʿ

Cf. the discussion of this name under AS 58.

AS 55 (ca. 600; Herr 1978: 72; Vattioni 1969: no. 170)

lʾlʿz // bn ʿzrʾl

Herr identifies this paleographically as a "probable Ammonite seal," because the letters diverge somewhat from the regular Ammonite forms. For *ʾlʿz*, cf. AS 32.

AS 56 (ca. 600; Herr 1978: 73; Vattioni 1969: no. 146)

lyšʿ // ʿdʾl

Identified as "possible Ammonite" by "process of elimination" (Herr 1978: 73).

AS 57 (slightly later than 600; Herr 1978: 63; Vattioni 1969: no. 116)

lʿnmwt ʾ//mt dblbs

Both names on this seal are difficult, but only the first requires examination in this study, because it has an internal *waw*. There are no parallels to it in the Canaanite onomasticon, but a cognate is attested in an inscription from Palmyra, *ʿnmw* (Stark 1971: 106). Though the language of that inscription is Aramaic, the name is Arabic, from *ǵānim*, "successful, noble" (Stark 1971: 106). In pre-Islamic Arabic inscriptions, the names *ʿnm*, *ʿnmt*, *ǵnm*, and *ǵnmt* have been found, as well as other names which also contain *ʿnm/ǵnm* (Harding 1971: 445, 458–59; Jackson 1983). In the Palmyrene example, the name is masculine. The final *taw* in the name from our Ammonite seal reflects the fact that it is a feminine name (cf. *mnḥmt*, Vattioni 1969: 367, and *mnḥm*, AS 1, 3, 38; also the pairs *ʿnm/ʿnmt* and *ǵnm/ǵnmt*, cited above). It has been pointed out elsewhere that some names on Ammonite seals have Arabic cognates (Garbini 1970; 1972: 97–103; 1974: 163–65; Jackson 1983). However, the vast majority of the Ammonite names are clearly Canaanite, as is the language in which the texts were written.

The vocalization of the medial *waw* in *ʿnmwt* is uncertain. It possibly is *ū*, in a feminine ending *ūt*. Other options cannot be ruled out, including reading it as a consonant.

AS 58 (early 6th century; Herr 1978: 61)

l'lyšʿ // bn grgr

The first name is vocalized either **'ilyašaʿ* or **'ilîšaʿ*. The former pronunciation assumes a construction *'l* + the verb *yšʿ* in the perfect (cf. *'lyṯʿ* in Liḥyanite, Harding 1971: 73, and the other cognates listed in Jackson 1983: s.v. *'lyšʿ*). This type of construction (*'il* + perfect verb) is common in the Ammonite onomasticon and also in Biblical Hebrew. Yet the Biblical Hebrew examples of *'lyšʿ* are vocalized *'ĕlîšāʿ* by the Massoretes, patterned after the even more common (in Biblical Hebrew) construction of *'ĕlî* + noun or adjective (1 Kgs 19:16, etc.). Cf. the LXX rendering *Elisa*.

The notable feature of this word, if the vocalization **'ilîšaʿ* is correct, would be the *mater lectionis yod*. This spelling contrasts to that of the same name in AS 44, which dates, according to Herr's analysis (1978: 60–61), to a slightly earlier period. *'lyšʿ* is found also in AS 46, which dates to the same period as AS 44. It is not impossible that this name could be attested both with and without the orthographic representation of the vowel in the late 7th century B.C.

AS 59 (early 6th century; Herr 1978: 64; Vattioni 1971: no. 261)

lšwḥr // hnss

The name *šwḥr* requires comment because of the *waw*. According to Garbini (1972: 101), it is an Arabic name (cf. AS 57) and derives from the verbal root *s_1ḥr* (viz., Classical Arabic *saḥara*, "to charm"; cf. *saḥar*, "dawn"). The name is well attested in pre-Islamic Arabian inscriptions (Jackson 1983), but it also appears three times in Judahite seals (Herr 1978: 97, 98). Avigad takes it from *šḥr*, meaning "look diligently for, seek" (cf. Ps 78:34, where *šḥr* is used in parallel construction with *drš*), and reads it as a participial-type name (1970: 287). Naveh (1965: 80) also suggests that it is a participial name and classifies it with such names as *šwmr* (*šômēr*, 1 Chr 7:32) and *ʿwbd* (*ʿôbēd*, Ruth 4:17). In contrast, Cross suggests that the name is a diminutive rather than a participle (personal communication). The three examples of *šḥr* from Judahite seals, mentioned above, are all spelled without the internal *waw*, as, of course, are all of the Arabic examples. If our present specimen is in fact the same name, then the *waw* is a *mater lectionis*. Cf. the additional comments in the orthographic discussion, below.

The second word, *nss*, probably is a noun meaning "standard bearer," or the like (cf. BH *nēs*, "standard"), as has been suggested by Avigad (1970: 287). Note the standard Canaanite definite article *h*-, which already has been identified in Ammonite from the Tell Siran inscription. Several other seals have this type of professional identification, consisting of the definite article *h*- followed by the title: e.g., *hspr*, "the scribe" (Moabite; Herr 1978: 154, 156) and *hṣrp*, "the goldsmith" (Diringer 1934: no. 102).

AS 60 (6th century; Avigad 1977b: 109)

lḥn' bn // byd'l

The name *ḥn'*, **ḥana'*, bears the hypocoristic ending *'alep*. For *byd'l*, cf. the discussion under the same name in AS 6.

AS 61 (5th century; Avigad 1977b: 109)

lbyd'l // bn 'lmg

Lexicon

'mt	nf (52, 57 = cstr) servant (f)
b-	prep (49) in
bn	nm (1, 3, 7 obv and rev, 8, 9, 10, 11, 12, 14, 16, 17, 22, 25, 27 obv, 28, 29, 32, 34, 37, 38 obv, 41, 44, 45, 46, 47, 55, 58, 60, 61 = cstr) son
brk	vb (36 = *Qal* pass pcp ms; 49 = tbrkh, *Pi'el* impf 3fs + 3ms sfx h) bless
bt	nf (40, 51 = cstr) daughter
h-	def art (59) the
ḥtm	nm (36 = cstr) seal
l-	prep (1, 3, 4, 5, 6, 7 obv and rev, 8, 9, 10, 11, 12, 13, 15, 16, 17, 18, 19, 20, 21, 22, 23, 24, 25, 26, 27 obv and rev, 28, 29, 30, 32, 33, 34, 35, 36, 37, 38 obv and rev, 39, 40, 41, 42, 44, 45, 46, 47, 49, 50, 51, 52, 53, 54, 55, 56, 57, 58, 59, 60, 61) (belonging) to
mlk	nm (17) king
ndr	vb (49 = *Qal* pf 3ms) vow
nss	nm (59) standard bearer (?)
n'r	nm (50, 53 = cstr) servant, young man
'bd	nm (6, 17, 18, 19 = cstr) servant (m)
š-	rel prn (49) which

Personal Names

'byḥy	(40)
'bndb	(49)
'dnnr	(18)
'dnplṭ	(19)
'w'	(47)
'l'	(14)
'l'wr	(34)
'l'mṣ	(44)
'l'mt	(34)
'lybr	(38 obv and rev)

'lydn	(11)
'ly'm	(20)
'lyš'	(46, 54, 58)
'lmg	(61)
'lmšl	(42)
'lndb	(11)
'lntn	(29)
'l'z	(32, 55)
'l'zr	(37)
'lrm	(50)
'lšgb	(51)
'lšm'	(5, 27 obv and rev, 33, 51)
'lš'	(44)
'ltmk	(22)
'mr'l	(45)
bd'l	(7 obv and rev)
bṭš	(53)
byd'l	(6, 60, 61)
b'r'	(27 obv)
bqš	(41)
brk'l	(53)
grgr	(58)
dblbs	(57)
ḥṭš	(8, 14)
ḥn'	(60)
ḥnn'l	(52)
ym̊n	(1)
ynḥm	(40, 45)
yš'	(56)
yš''l	(48)
ytyr	(29)
mgr'l	(28)
mkm'l	(35)
mng'nrt	(36)
mnḥm	(1, 3, 17, 28, 32, 38)
mnr	(30)
mqnmlk	(10)
mr'l	(47)
mr'	(21)

ndb’l	(7 obv and rev, 12, 25, 37, 41)
smk	(17)
‘bd	(39)
‘bd’	(50)
‘d’l	(56)
‘zr’l	(55)
‘lyh	(52)
‘mndb	(18, 19)
‘ms’l	(4, 12, 22)
‘nmwt	(57)
‘šn’l	(2)
pd’l	(6, 43)
plṭ	(26)
plṭw	(9)
plṭy	(16)
šb’l	(15)
šwḥr	(59)
šm‘	(13, 23)
šm‘l	(9)
š‘l	(46)
tmk[	(10)
tmk’	(25)
tmk’l	(16, 24)
tnḥm	(3)

Divine Names

mlkm	(36)
‘št<rt>	(49)

Place Name

ṣdn	(49)

Morphology

1. *Nouns*

a) Attested forms:

’mt (52, 57)	fs cstr
bn (1, 3, 7 obv and	ms cstr

rev, 8, 9, 10, 11,
12, 14, 16, 17,
22, 25, 27 obv,
28, 29, 32, 34,
37, 38 obv, 41,
44, 45, 46, 47,
55, 58, 60, 61)

bt (40, 51)	fs cstr
ḥtm (36)	ms cstr
mlk (17)	ms
nss (59)	ms
n‘r (50, 53)	ms cstr
‘bd (6, 17, 18, 19)	ms cstr

b) Inflections:

ms:	mlk	-∅
	nss	-∅
ms cstr:	bn	-∅
	ḥtm	-∅
	n‘r	-∅
	‘bd	-∅
fs cstr:	’mt	-t (-at)
	bt	-t (-at)

2. *Verbs*

a) Attested forms:

brk (36)	*Qal* pass pcp ms
tbrk (49)	*Pi‘el* impf 3fs
ndr (49)	*Qal* pf 3ms

b) Conjugations:

Qal

perfect:

3ms	ndr	- - -

passive participle:

ms	brk	- - -

Pi‘el

imperfect:

3fs	tbrk	t- - -

3. *Prepositions*

b- (49)

l- (1, 3, 4, 5, 6, 7 obv and rev, 8, 9, 10, 11, 12, 13, 15, 16, 17, 18, 19, 20, 21, 22, 23, 24, 25, 26, 27 obv and rev, 28, 29, 30, 32, 33, 34, 35, 36, 37, 38 obv and rev, 39, 40, 41, 42, 44, 45, 46, 47, 49, 50, 51, 52, 53, 54, 55, 56, 57, 58, 59, 60, 61)

4. *Definite Article*

h- (59)

5. *Relative Pronoun*

š- (49)

6. *Pronominal Suffix*

3ms -h (49)

Summary

The morphology of the Ammonite seals identifies their language as a member of the Canaanite family.

a) *Nouns*: The inflection of the nouns, as far as is demonstrated in the seals, is identical to that of Hebrew, Moabite, and Phoenician: ms (-Ø), ms cstr (-Ø), fs cstr (*-at*).

b) *Verbs, prepositions, and definite article*: The verbal conjugations, prepositions, and definite article also show no divergence from the patterns of those languages.

c) *Relative pronoun*: The relative pronoun *š*- agrees with Israelite and Mishnaic Hebrew but contrasts with Phoenician, where *'š* was used, and Judahite and Moabite, where *'šr* was used. Most significantly, it contrasts with the relative pronoun *'š* found in an Ammonite text from Heshbon (H 1.6). It is important to note that the seal where *š*- is found (AS 49) is enigmatic in other ways as well and may not have been written in Ammonite.

d) *Pronominal suffix*: The 3ms pronominal object suffix *-h* is found in the same seal. If the seal is Ammonite, then this is our only example of a 3ms suffix for this language. The same cautions should be demonstrated with regard to this datum as to the relative pronoun *š*- discussed above.

Phonology and Orthography

Most of the Ammonite seals fall within the boundaries of the 7th century B.C. The evidence which they provide is therefore limited to that one stage in the history of Ammonite scribal practice. In general, taking orthographic information from personal names—which make up the largest body of words in these seals—must be done with caution. Orthographic conclusions drawn from names cannot be applied uncritically to the language as a whole, since names often retain traditional features which do not reflect later linguistic or orthographic developments. Nonetheless, the information provided in the seals is helpful and does contribute to our understanding of the Ammonite spelling system.

Medial yod for ī

'byḥy (40), *'lybr* (38 obv and rev), *'lydn* (?) (11), and *'ly'm* (20). The use of *yod* to represent medial ī, the 1cs pronominal suffix in sentence names of this type, is the minority spelling. The defective spelling is twice as common: *'bndb* (49), *'dnnr* (18), *'dnplṭ* (19), *'l'wr* (34), *'l'mt* (34), *'l'z* (32, 55), *'lrm* (50), *'lš'* (44), and *'mndb* (18, 19). There is no chronological explanation for the differences in spelling. It appears that the use of *yod* to represent internal ī was not an established orthographic law in this period (cf. Cross and Freedman 1952: 57).

Medial waw for ū

'l'wr (34). The same name with identical spelling is found in H 3.5.

Final 'alep for a

'w' (47), *'l'* (14), *b'r'* (27 obv), *ḥn'* (60), *'bd'* (50), and *tmk'* (25). The hypocoristic termination *'alep* is relatively common in Ammonite; cf. also *gn'* (NO 6) and *'z'* (NO 4).

Final yod for ī

plṭy (16). Cf. also *bnny* (H 3.11) and *ḥgy* (NO 13).

Final waw for ū

plṭw (9). Possibly representing *ō*, this hypocoristic ending is otherwise unattested in Ammonite. Final *waw* is also found in Arabic names in Palmyrene Aramaic inscriptions (Stark 1971).

Uncertain examples

ʿnmwt (57). The vocalization of the medial *waw* cannot be determined on the basis of this orthography. The same name is found spelled without *waw*—*ʿnmt* and *ǵnmt*—in Safaitic (Harding 1971: 445–58). This may suggest that the *waw* represents a vowel, probably *ū*.

ʿlyh (52). The interpretation of this name is uncertain, but it is not impossible that the final *he* represents *ā*. The *yod* is undoubtedly consonantal.

šwḥr (59). Naveh (1965: 80) reads this name as a participle. The *ō* in Canaanite participles comes from an original *ā* in Proto-Canaanite **qā́tilu* forms (Bauer and Leander 1922: #43*n*). If *šwḥr* is in fact a participle, then the *mater lectionis waw*, representing *ō* < *ā́*, is unique in all of Northwest Semitic for this period. But the interpretation of the name is still problematic.

tbrkh (49). For the phonology and orthography of the final *he*, cf. the discussion of AS 49. I am inclined to vocalize it as -*ō*, with Phoenician. Cf. Cross (1974: 494), who reconstructs Ammonite phonology on the basis of Phoenician, rather than Hebrew, because of other Phoenician/Ammonite isoglosses. The *he* would not be a *mater lectionis*, but a historical spelling.

Summary

The evidence for internal *matres lectionis* is mixed; the majority of internal long vowels are not represented in the orthography. This reflects both orthographic fluidity and the conservative character of names orthographically.

All final vowels in the seals, as far as can be identified, are represented.

Word Division

Word dividers are almost nonexistent in Ammonite seals, used consistently in seal 52 and only inconsistently in seals 18 and 36.

Linguistic Affiliation of the Ammonite Seals

There is nothing in this corpus of seals to suggest that the language in which they were written is not Ammonite. The lexicon includes words which are thoroughly attested in Hebrew, Moabite, and Phoenician. The only exception is *nss*, unknown in this form, but likely related to the Hebrew noun *nēs*. For the relative pronoun *š*-, which is extremely important for comparative dialectology in Canaanite, see the extensive discussion of, and the problems relating to, AS 49, above. The morphology of the language of the seals is also consistent with what already has been observed in Ammonite inscriptions.

CHAPTER EIGHT

THE AMMONITE LANGUAGE: SYNTHESIS AND SUMMATION

The following lists contain all of the elements of Ammonite lexicon and grammar known as of this date.

The Ammonite Lexicon

’kl	nm (H 1.1, 4 [?], 8, 9) food, grain
’l	nm (AC 6 = ’lm, pl) god
’mt	nf (AS 52, 57 = cstr) servant (f)
’rḥ	nf (H 1.5, 11) cow
’š	rel prn (H 1.6) which, that
’šḥt	nf (TS 5 = fpl) cisterns (?)
’tḥr	n (TS 4) (?)
b-	prep (AC 4, 6; TS 7; AS 49) in, among, for
bn	nm (TS 2, 3; H 1.3; 3.2, 3, 4, 7, 8, 9, 10; 5.1, 3, 4; NO 1, 2, 3, 4, 5, 6, 7, 8, 9, 10, 11, 12, 13; AS 1, 3, 7 obv and rev, 8, 9, 10, 11, 12, 14, 16, 17, 22, 25, 27 obv, 28, 29, 32, 34, 37, 38 obv, 41, 44, 45, 46, 47, 55, 58, 60, 61 = cstr; AC 6; TS 1, 2, 3; AT 2 = pl cstr) son
bny	vb (AC 1 = bnh, *Qal* imv ms; AT 1 = ’bnh, *Qal* impf 1cs) build
bʿr	nm (H 2.3 = bʿrm, pl) beast of burden
brk	vb (AS 36 = *Qal* pass pcp ms; 49 = tbrkh, *Piʿel* impf 3fs + 3ms sfx -h) bless
bt	nf (H 1.5, 11; AS 40, 51 = cstr) daughter
gyl	vb (TS 6 = ygl, *Qal* juss 3ms) rejoice
gnt	nf (TS 4) garden
dš’	nm (H 1.9) grass, hay
h	def art (TS 4 = h; TS 4bis; AS 59 = h-) the
w-	conj (AC 3, 4, 7bis, 8; TS 4bis, 5, 6, 7; H 1.2, 3, 5, 7, 8) and

ḥbl nm (H 2.4 = ḥblm, pl) rope
ḥtm nm (AS 36 = cstr) seal
ywm nm (TS 7 = ywmt, fpl) day
yn nm (H 1.7, 8) wine
k- prep (AC 2) like, as, according to
kbs vb (NO 14 = *Qal* act pcp ms) wash, launder
kḥd vb (AC 3 = h]kḥd, *Hip'il* inf abs; 'kḥd, *Hip'il* impf 1cs) destroy, annihilate
kl nm (AC 2, 3, 4 = cstr) all
ksp nm (H 1.6) silver, silver piece
krm nm (TS 4) vineyard
l- prep (AC 1, 8 = lk, l + 2ms sfx -k; H 1.3, 4, 5, 6bis, 9; 3.1; AS 1, 3, 4, 5, 6, 7 obv and rev, 8, 9, 10, 11, 12, 13, 15, 16, 17, 18, 19, 20, 21, 22, 23, 24, 25, 26, 27 obv and rev, 28, 29, 30, 32, 33, 34, 35, 36, 37, 38 obv and rev, 39, 40, 41, 42, 44, 45, 46, 47, 49, 50, 51, 52, 53, 54, 55, 56, 57, 58, 59, 60, 61) to, for, (belonging) to
lbbt nf (H 1.7 = lbbt, fpl) loaf, cake
lyn vb (AC 4 = ylnn, *Qal* impf 3mpl) dwell, remain
m- prep (H 1.3, 4) from
mb'(t) n (AC 1 = mb't, fpl) entrance
mwt vb (AC 2 = mt, *Qal* inf abs; ymtn, *Qal* impf 3mpl) die
mlk nm (H 1.1; AS 17 = abs; TS 1, 2, 3 = cstr) king
m'bd nm (TS 1 = pl cstr) work
ndr vb (AS 49 = *Qal* pf 3ms) vow
nk't nf (H 1.4, 5) a gum or spice
nss nm (AS 59) standard bearer (?)
n'r nm (AS 50, 53 = cstr) servant, young man
ntn vb (H 1.6 = *Qal* pf 3ms) give
sbb vb (AC 2 = msbb, *Po'el* pcp ms) surround
sbbt prep (AC 1) around
sd̊rt nf (AC 4) chamber, hall, colonnade (?)
'bd nm (AS 6, 17, 18, 19 = cstr) servant (m)
'l- prep (AC 2 = 'lk, 'l + 2ms sfx -k) upon
'rb vb (AC 3 = m'rb, *Hip'il* [?] pcp ms) enter (?)
ṣ'n nm (H 1.2, 7, 10) small cattle
ṣdq̊ nm (AC 4 = ṣdq̊[m, mpl) just one, righteous one (?)

rb	adj (TS 7 = rbm, mpl) many, much
rḥq	adj (TS 8 = rḥqt, fpl) distant, far off
š-	rel prn (AS 49) which
šlm	nm (AC 8) completeness, well-being, peace
šmḥ	vb (TS 6 = yšmḥ, *Qal* juss 3ms) be glad, be happy
š(n)t	nf (TS 7 = šnt, fpl) year
št'	vb (AC 6 = tšt', *Qal* impf 2ms) fear
t'n	nm (H 2.1, 2) fig

Personal Names in Ammonite Inscriptions

'byḥy	(AS 40)
'bndb	(AS 49)
'dnnr	(AS 18)
'dnplṭ	(AS 19)
'w'	(AS 47)
'yndb	(NO 13)
'l'	(AS 14)
'l'wr	(H 3.5; AS 34)
'l'mṣ	(AS 44)
'l'mt	(AS 34)
'lybr	(AS 38 obv and rev)
'lydn	(AS 11)
'ly'm	(AS 20)
'lyš'	(NO 11; AS 46, 54, 58)
'lmg	(AS 61)
'lmšl	(AS 42)
'lndb	(H 3.6; AS 11)
'lnr	(NO 7, 8, 12)
'lntn	(AS 29)
'l'z	(AS 32, 55)
'l'zr	(H 3.4; AS 37)
'lrm	(H 3.2; AS 50)
'lšgb	(AS 51)
'lšm'	(AS 5, 27 obv and rev, 33, 51)
'lš'	(AS 44)
'ltmk	(NO 14; AS 22)
'mr'l	(AS 45)
bd'l	(AS 7 obv and rev)

btš	(AS 53)
byd'l	(NO 3; AS 6, 60, 61)
blntn	(NO 15)
bnny	(H 3.11)
b'r'	(AS 27 obv)
b'š['	(H 1.6)
bqš	(AS 41)
brk'l	(AS 53)
brq	(H 3.6)
gn'	(NO 6)
grgr	(AS 58)
dblbs	(AS 57)
hṣl'l	(TS 2)
zkr'l	(NO 9)
ḥgy	(NO 13)
ḥz'l	(NO 5)
ḥṭš	(AS 8, 14)
ḥmšgb	(H 3.7)
ḥn'	(AS 60)
ḥnn	(NO 10)
ḥnn'l	(NO 2, 5; AS 52)
ym̊n	(AS 1)
ynḥm	(AS 40, 45)
yš'	(AS 56)
yš''l	(AS 48)
ytb	(H 1.9)
ytyr	(AS 29)
mgr'l	(AS 28)
mḥm	(NO 7)
m]k'l	(NO 12)
mkm'l	(AS 35)
m̊lk'l	(H 3.4)
mng'nrt	(AS 36)
mnḥm	(NO 3, 6, 11; AS 1, 3, 17, 28, 32, 38)
mnr	(AS 30)
mqnmlk	(AS 10)
mr'l	(AS 47)
mr'	(AS 21)

ndb'l	(H 1.3; NO 10; AS 7 obv and rev, 12, 25, 37, 41)
nnydn	(H 5.5)
n'm'l	(H 1.3)
nqr	(H 3.5)
n]tn'l	(H 6)
smk	(AS 17)
'bd	(AS 39)
'bd'	(AS 50)
'd'l	(AS 56)
'z'	(NO 4)
'zy'[l	(H 5.2)
'zr'l	(H 3.3; AS 55)
'kbr	(NO 15)
'lyh	(AS 52)
'mndb	(TS 1, 3; AS 18, 19)
'ms'l	(AS 4, 12, 22)
'n'l	(NO 1, 2)
'nmwt	(AS 57)
'qb	(H 3.10)
'šn'l	(AS 2)
pd'l	(AS 6, 43)
plṭ	(AS 26)
plṭw	(AS 9)
plṭy	(AS 16)
psmy	(H 5.4)
pr̊š	(H 3.7)
ṣnr	(NO 9)
rp'	(H 5.3)
šb'l	(NO 4; AS 15)
šwḥr	(AS 59)
šm'	(AS 13, 23)
šm'l	(AS 9)
šm̊š'l	(H 3.8)
š'l	(AS 46)
šql	(H 3.9)
tmk[	(AS 10)
tmk'	(AS 25)
tmk'l	(H 4.3; AS 16, 24)

tnḥm	(AS 3)

Divine Names in Ammonite Inscriptions

mlkm	(AC 1; AS 36)
‘št<rt>	(AS 49)

Place Names in Ammonite Inscriptions

’lt	(H 1.4)
ḥ̊š̊[b]n̊	(H 3.1)
‘mn	(TS 1, 2, 3; AT 2)
ṣdn	(AS 49)

Ammonite Morphology

1. *Nouns and Adjectives*

a) Attested forms:

’kl (H 1.1, 4 [?], 8, 9)	ms
’lm (AC 6)	mpl
’mt (AS 52, 57)	fs cstr
’rḥ (H 1.5, 11)	fs
’šḥt (TS 5)	fpl (?)
’tḥr (TS 4)	ms (?)
bn (TS 2, 3; H 1.3; 3.2, 3, 4, 7, 8, 9, 10; 5.1, 3, 4; NO 1, 2, 3, 4, 5, 6, 7, 8, 9, 10, 11, 12, 13; AS 1, 3, 7 obv and rev, 8, 9, 10, 11, 12, 14, 16, 17, 22, 25, 27 obv, 28, 29, 32, 34, 37, 38 obv, 41, 44, 45, 46, 47, 55, 58, 60, 61)	ms cstr
bn (AC 6; TS 1, 2, 3; AT 2)	mpl cstr

b'rm (H 2.3)	mpl
bt (H 1.5, 11; AS 40, 51)	fs cstr
gnt (TS 4)	fs
dš' (H 1.9)	ms
ḥblm (H 2.4)	mpl
ḥtm (AS 36)	ms cstr
ywmt (TS 7)	fpl
yn (H 1.7, 8)	ms
kl (AC 2, 3, 4)	ms cstr
ksp (H 1.6)	ms
krm (TS 4)	ms
lbbt (H 1.7)	fpl
mb't (AC 1)	fpl
mlk (H 1.1; AS 17)	ms
mlk (TS 1, 2, 3)	ms cstr
m'bd (TS 1)	mpl cstr
nk't (H 1.4, 5)	fs
nss (AS 59)	ms
n'r (AS 50, 53)	ms cstr
s̊drt (AC 4)	fs (?)
'bd (AS 6, 17, 18, 19)	ms cstr
ṣ'n (H 1.2, 7, 10)	ms
ṣdq̊[m (AC 4)	mpl (?)
rbm (TS 7)	mpl
rḥqt (TS 8)	fpl
šlm (AC 8)	ms
šnt (TS 7)	fpl
t'n (H 2.1, 2)	ms

b) Inflections:

ms:	'kl	-Ø
	'tḥr (?)	-Ø
	dš'	-Ø
	yn	-Ø
	ksp	-Ø
	krm	-Ø
	mlk	-Ø
	nss	-Ø

	ṣ'n	-∅
	šlm	-∅
	t'n	-∅
ms cstr:	bn	-∅
	ḥtm	-∅
	kl	-∅
	mlk	-∅
	n'r	-∅
	'bd	-∅
mpl:	'lm	-m (-īm)
	b'rm	-m (-īm)
	ḥblm	-m (-īm)
	rbm	-m (-īm)
mpl cstr:	bn	-∅ (-ē)
	m'bd	-∅ (-ē)
fs:	'rḥ	-∅
	gnt	-t (-at)
	nk't	-t (-at)
	s̊drt (?)	-t (-at)
fs cstr:	'mt	-t (-at)
	bt	-t (-at)
fpl:	'šḥt (?)	-t (-ōt)
	ywmt	-t (-ōt)
	lbbt	-t (-ōt)
	mb't	-t (-ōt)
	rḥqt	-t (-ōt)
	šnt	-t (-ōt)
fpl cstr:	no attested forms	

2. *Verbs*

a) Attested forms:

bnh (AC 1)	*Qal* imv ms
'bnh (AT 1)	*Qal* impf 1cs
brk (AS 36)	*Qal* pass pcp ms
tbrk (AS 49)	*Pi'el* impf 3fs
ygl (TS 6)	*Qal* juss 3ms
kbs (NO 14)	*Qal* act pcp ms
h]kḥd (AC 3)	*Hip'il* inf abs (perhaps *Qal*?)
'kḥd (AC 3)	*Hip'il* impf 1cs (perhaps *Qal*?)

ylnn (AC 4)	*Qal* impf 3mpl
mt (AC 2)	*Qal* inf abs
ymtn (AC 2)	*Qal* impf 3mpl
ndr (AS 49)	*Qal* pf 3ms
ntn (H 1.6)	*Qal* pf 3ms
msbb (AC 2)	*Po'el* pcp ms
m'rb (AC 3)	*Hip'il* pcp ms
yšmḥ (TS 6)	*Qal* juss 3ms
tšt' (AC 6)	*Qal* impf 2ms

b). Conjugations:

Qal

perfect:

3ms	ndr	- - -
	ntn	- - -

imperfect:

1cs	'bnh	'- - -
2ms	tšt'	t- - -
3mpl	ylnn	y- - -n
	ymtn	y- - -n

imperative:

ms	bnh	- - -

infinitive absolute:

	mt	- - -

jussive:

3ms	ygl	y- - -
	yšmḥ	y- - -

active participle:

ms	kbs	- - -

passive participle:

ms	brk	- - -

Pi'el

imperfect:

3fs	tbrk	t- - -

Po'el

participle:

ms	msbb	m- - -

Hip'il

imperfect:

1cs	'kḥd	'- - -

participle:

ms	m'rb	m- - -

3. *Prepositions*

b-	(AC 4, 6; TS 7; AS 49)
k-	(AC 2)
l-	(AC 1, 8; H 1.3, 4, 5, 6bis, 9; 3.1; AS 1, 3, 4, 5, 6, 7 obv and rev, 8, 9, 10, 11, 12, 13, 15, 16, 17, 18, 19, 20, 21, 22, 23, 24, 25, 26, 27 obv and rev, 28, 29, 30, 32, 33, 34, 35, 36, 37, 38 obv and rev, 39, 40, 41, 42, 44, 45, 46, 47, 49, 50, 51, 52, 53, 54, 55, 56, 57, 58, 59, 60, 61)
m-	(H 1.3, 4)
sbbt	(AC 1)
'l-	(AC 2)

4. *Definite Article*

h	(TS 4)
h-	(TS 4bis; AS 59)

5. *Conjunction*

w-	(AC 3, 4, 7bis, 8; TS 4bis, 5, 6, 7; H 1.2, 3, 5, 7, 8)

6. *Relative Pronouns*

'š	(H 1.6)
š-	(AS 49)

7. *Pronominal Suffixes*

2ms	-k	(AC 1, 2, 8)
3ms	-h	(AS 49)

Summary

a) *Nouns and adjectives*: The inflectional endings of nouns and adjectives attested in Ammonite inscriptions identify the following combinations of number, gender, and state: ms (-Ø), ms cstr (-Ø), mpl (-*īm*), mpl cstr (-*ē*), fs (-Ø), fs (-*at*), fs cstr (-*at*), and fpl (-*ōt*). The fpl cstr is unattested, and there are no recognizable dual forms.

b) *Verbs*: Ammonite preserves a variety of verbal forms, but considering the large amount of stems and conjugations extant in Northwest Semitic, the Ammonite corpus is quite limited: *Qal* perfect 3ms; imperfect 1cs, 2ms, 3mpl; imperative ms; infinitive absolute; jussive 3ms; active participle ms; passive participle ms; *Piʿel* imperfect 3fs; *Poʿel* participle ms; *Hipʿil* imperfect 1cs; participle ms. In addition to these forms, a Gt stem has been suggested by Krahmalkov (1976: 56) for *ʾtḥr*, TS 4 (cf. chap. 3, Philological Comments). Regrettably there are no examples of the *Nipʿal* stem.

c) *Prepositions, definite article, conjunction*: The prepositions *b*-, *k*-, *l*-, *m*-, and *ʿl* are all common throughout Canaanite. *sbbt*, which is used in AC 1 as a preposition, as often in Hebrew, is attested in the Bible. The Ammonite definite article is *h*- (note the one occurrence of *h*, TS 4); the conjunction *w*- is common to all of Northwest Semitic.

d) *Pronouns*: Pronouns are scarce in Ammonite. There are no independent pronouns, demonstrative pronouns, or interrogative pronouns. This is unfortunate, as these words would aid considerably in the process of classifying Ammonite among the other languages of Iron Age Syria-Palestine. For example, the 1st person independent pronouns in Biblical Hebrew are *ʾănî* and *ʾānōkî*, Moabite *ʾnk*, Phoenician *ʾnk*, and Aramaic *ʾnh*. An Ammonite example would provide a valuable isogloss. The Ammonite pronoun suffixes are also limited: 2ms is -*k*; 3ms is -*h*. Two relative pronouns are attested, *ʾš* (H 1.6) and *š*- (AS 49).

Ammonite Phonology and Orthography

The greatest difficulty encountered in the study of Northwest Semitic orthography is that of determining to what extent the phonology of a given language can be reconstructed using as evidence the orthographic system employed in the texts. This problem is especially important because the alphabetic writing system used in Northwest Semitic inscriptions originally represented only consonants (Albright 1966; Cross and Freedman

1952: 9, 58; cf. Cross 1979: 97–111) and even later used vowel letters sparingly or not at all (Cross and Freedman 1952: 11–60). The addition of letters to represent vowel sounds took place later in specific situations. Vowel letters can be divided into two categories. They are termed "historical spellings" if they are vestiges of earlier spellings which remained in the system after phonetic changes had removed the consonantal phonemes which they originally represented (e.g., *yod* for *ē* [< *ay*]). *Matres lectionis* are graphemes, used to represent vowels, which have no etymological relationship to the vowels which they represent (e.g., Biblical Hebrew *šālôm*, with *waw* representing *ō*). The distinction between these two types of vowel letters is important only as it sheds light on the historical development of the phonology and the orthographic system.

According to Cross and Freedman (1952: 58–60), *matres lectionis* were first invented by the Arameans shortly after they borrowed the alphabet from the Phoenicians (ca. 11th–10th centuries B.C.). They were used originally only in final position but later were applied internally as well. This system, in turn, was adopted by Hebrew and Moabite scribes, beginning in the 9th century. Recently, much attention has focused on the use of vowel letters in Ugaritic and the possibility of the Ugaritic system being the source for the use of *matres lectionis* in the later linear scripts (e.g., Zevit 1980: 1–10 and references there). Ugaritic scribes occasionally used graphemes which under normal conditions represented consonants to represent vowels. This was not done in a highly developed consistent system, but the presence of *matres lectionis* in Ugaritic texts does demonstrate that the idea of representing vowels in a normally consonantal writing system existed in the eastern Mediterranean in the 2nd millennium B.C. (Zevit 1980: 3–5). The paucity of evidence makes it impossible to determine if or to what extent this Ugaritic development could have influenced Iron Age Canaanite scribal practice.

The origin of *matres lectionis* is far outside of the scope of the present study and need not be pursued further here. It should be pointed out, however, that the earliest extant Ammonite text, the Citadel inscription, demonstrates that the scribes of Ammon had adopted the use of *matres lectionis*, at least to a limited degree, by the mid-9th century (*bnh*, line 1).

My goal in analyzing Ammonite orthography—both independently of and in light of the systems used for other languages—has been twofold: (a) to identify the orthographic system employed by Ammonite scribes to represent the sounds of their language, and (b) to isolate features which are indicative of Ammonite phonology. These goals have been achieved only insofar as the Ammonite evidence presents clear and unambiguous examples.

The following data summarize information already presented in chaps. 2–7. For further discussion, cf. the orthographic and phonological comments there.

General orthographic features

In Ammonite the proto-Canaanite diphthong *ay* had contracted generally to *ē*: *bn*, **banē* (AC 6; TS 1, 2, 3; AT 2); *mʿbd*, **maʿbadē* (TS 1); *yn*, **yēn* (H 1.7, 8); *ʿlk*, **ʿalēk* (AC 2). In contrast, *aw* probably remained uncontracted: *ywmt*, **yawmōt* (TS 7).

The vowel *ē* (< *ay*) is never represented orthographically internally (*yn*: H 1.7, 8; *ʿlk*: AC 2) or in final position (*bn*: AC 6; TS 1, 2, 3; AT 2; *mʿbd*: TS 1).

The 2ms suffix is *-k* in Ammonite: *lk* (AC 1, 8); *ʿlk* (AC 2). Although the evidence is not conclusive, the spelling does suggest that no final vowel was present on this morpheme in Ammonite and that it was vocalized **-ak* (cf. Phonology and Orthography in chap. 2 and the references cited there).

Medial waw for ū

ʾlʾwr (H 3.5; AS 34).

ʿnmwt (AS 57). The *waw* probably represents *ū*. Cf. the discussion in chap. 7.

Medial waw

šwḥr (AS 59). Vocalization not known. Cf. the discussion in chap. 7.

Medial yod for ī

ʾbyḥy (AS 40), *ʾlybr* (AS 38 obv and rev), *ʾlyʿm* (AS 20), and *ʿzyʾ[l* (H 5.2). This represents the minority spelling. The defective spelling of medial ī is more than twice as common.

Final 'alep for a

Only in hypocoristic names: *'w'* (AS 47), *'l'* (AS 14), *b'r'* (AS 27 obv), *gn'* (NO 6), *ḥn'* (AS 60), *'bd'* (AS 50), *'z'* (NO 4), and *tmk'* (AS 25).

Final he for ē

bnh (AC 1) and *'bnh* (AT 1). For the phonology and orthography of ē, cf. chap. 4.

Final he for ō

tbrkh (AS 49). 3ms object suffix, probably ō < ū < *uhu*. The *he* is historical. Cf. the discussion in chap. 7.

Final he for ā (?)

'lyh (AS 52). Probably *ā*. Cf. the discusssion in chap. 7.

Final yod for ī

bnny (H 3.11), *ḥgy* (NO 13), *plṭy* (AS 16), and *psmy* (H 5.4), all hypocoristic endings on names.

Final waw for u (?)

plṭw (AS 9). Cf. the discussion in chap. 7.

Summary

Although not all examples are free from ambiguities, our evidence shows that all final vowels in Ammonite were represented orthographically, either with historical spellings or *matres lectionis*. These include *a* represented by *'alep* and possibly *he*, ī represented by *yod*, ē represented by *he*, probably also ō represented by *he*, and possibly *u* represented by *waw*.

Medial vowel letters are found only in names, and only inconsistently and infrequently there. These include *waw* for *ū* and *yod* for ī.

Word Division in Ammonite Inscriptions

Consistent word division cannot be listed as a characteristic trait of Ammonite texts. AS 52 is consistent in its use of dividers, and the Nimrud ostracon is almost consistent. The Citadel inscription uses dividers in over two-thirds of the expected locations (cf. chap. 2), but most of the other texts use them only sporadically—and with no apparent pattern—or not at all. Word division clearly was an optional practice among Ammonite scribes.

Linguistic Affiliation of Ammonite

In recent publications, G. Garbini (1970; updated and republished in 1972: 97–108; 1974: 159–68) has proposed that the Ammonite language does not belong to the group of languages which traditionally are called "Canaanite" (i.e., Ugaritic, Hebrew, Moabite, Phoenician). Parting with all of the other commentators mentioned in the introductions to the texts (chaps. 2–7), who see Ammonite as a Canaanite language, he states that it is "nearer to what we know as North Arabic than to the so-called 'Canaanite'" (1974: 163). In my view, this conclusion flies in the face of the evidence presented throughout this study, which demonstrates clearly that Ammonite belongs to the Canaanite family. Texts discovered since Garbini's publications further bear this out.

Garbini's conclusions are based in large part on the presence in Ammonite seals of personal names with cognates in Arabic. These occur occasionally, as was pointed out in chap. 7. As was stated by G. M. Landes in his study of Ammonite history and culture (1961: 84), the kingdom of Ammon maintained close ties with the desert and its peoples throughout all of the early Iron Age—much more so than did Edom or Moab. Albright (1953: 133) suggested that much of the caravan traffic from Arabia to the west was controlled by the Ammonites. Yet the relationship between the Ammonites and their Arab neighbors may have gone beyond commerce. The names seem to indicate that there was a substantial enough Arab population in Ammon—or contact with Arab population—that Arabic names were in occasional use. Even so, it must be pointed out that the overwhelming majority of the names found on Ammonite seals are Canaanite (Jackson 1983).

The presence of Arabic names in Ammonite epigraphs cannot alone identify Ammonite with Arabic, especially in light of the philological information contained in the texts. The classification of the language itself can be accomplished only on the basis of the linguistic data.

As was shown in the discussions presented in chaps. 2–7, the linguistic data gleaned from the inscriptions do in fact identify Ammonite as a close relative of Phoenician, Moabite, Israelite, and Judahite.

Lexicon

Of the many words found in the Ammonite lexicon, only a few are not known from the Hebrew Bible, the largest corpus of information for 1st-millennium-B.C. Canaanite. Many are also attested in other Canaanite inscriptions (cf. the more detailed presentations in chaps. 2–7).

Morphology

The morphology of Ammonite is clearly that of a Canaanite language. The paradigm of nominal inflections (see above) is identical to that of Phoenician. This paradigm might well be called "Standard Canaanite"; it differs from Hebrew with the fs termination *-at*, rather than Hebrew *-â*, and it differs from Moabite with the mpl termination *-īm*, rather than Moabite *-īn*.

Classification within Canaanite

Much more difficult than the task of assigning Ammonite *to* the family of Canaanite is that of identifying its position *within* that group *vis-à-vis* the other languages. There is not enough evidence to do so conclusively. As has been pointed out throughout this study, most of the lexical items identified in Ammonite are found in the Hebrew Bible. This undoubtedly reflects a close affinity between Hebrew and Ammonite, but it also reflects the fact that we have much more data for Hebrew than for any other Canaanite language. Valuable isoglosses are provided by words such as *ntn* and *ʾš*. The verb *ntn* aligns Ammonite with Hebrew and Moabite against Phoenician, while the relative pronoun *ʾš* aligns Ammonite with Phoenician against Hebrew and Moabite. Cf. the fuller discussion of these examples under Linguistic Affiliation, chap. 5. The relative pronoun š- (AS 49) aligns Ammonite with Israelite and Mishnaic Hebrew.

As was mentioned above, the morphology of the Ammonite noun is identical to that of Phoenician, at least as far as can be ascertained from the writing system. Information concerning verbal conjugations is quite sketchy, and none of the attested forms contribute to the classification of Ammonite within Canaanite. As was pointed out in chap. 2, the final *nun* of the Ammonite 3mpl imperfects is known from Hebrew and Phoenician as well, though it is used consistently elsewhere only in Aramaic and Ugaritic.

Because the linguistic information provided by the Ammonite texts is so limited, both in quantity and in scope, it is, in my opinion, not possible to align Ammonite definitively either with Phoenician to the north, Israelite and Judahite to the west, or Moabite to the south. More unambiguous diagnostic features are needed before such a classification is possible. I believe that it is clear, however, that Ammonite had its own special features which distinguished it from the languages of neighboring peoples. To what extent that distinction existed, and the degree to which Ammonite resembled one language more than another, can only be known with certainty with the discovery of additional texts.

BIBLIOGRAPHY

Aharoni, Y.

1975 *Kĕtūbōt ʾărād*. Jerusalem: The Bialik Institute.

AHw

1959–81 *Akkadisches Handwörterbuch*. By W. von Soden. Wiesbaden: Otto Harrassowitz.

Albright, W. F.

1941 Ostracon No. 6043 from Ezion-Geber. *Bulletin of the American Schools of Oriental Research* 82: 11–15.

1953 Notes on Ammonite History. Pp. 131–36 in *Miscellanea Biblica B. Ubach*, ed. Romuald Maria Díaz Carbonell, O.S.B. Barcelona: Montisserrati.

1958 An Ostracon from Calah and the North-Israelite Diaspora. *Bulletin of the American Schools of Oriental Research* 149: 33–36.

1966 *The Proto-Sinaitic Inscriptions and Their Decipherment*. Harvard Theological Studies 22. Cambridge, MA: Harvard University.

1970 Some Comments on the ʿAmmân Citadel Inscription. *Bulletin of the American Schools of Oriental Research* 198: 38–40.

Andersen, F. I.

1966 Moabite Syntax. *Orientalia* 35: 81–120.

ANEP

1954 *The Ancient Near East in Pictures Relating to the Old Testament*. Ed. J. B. Pritchard. Princeton: Princeton University.

ANET

1969 *Ancient Near Eastern Texts Relating to the Old Testament*. Ed. J. B. Pritchard, 3d ed. with supplement. Princeton: Princeton University.

Avigad, N.

1966 Two Phoenician Votive Seals. *Israel Exploration Journal* 16: 243–51.

1970 Ammonite and Moabite Seals. Pp. 284–95 in *Near Eastern Archaeology in the Twentieth Century: Essays in Honor of Nelson Glueck*, ed. J. A. Sanders. Garden City, NY: Doubleday.

1977a Two Ammonite Seals Depicting the *Dea Nutrix*. *Bulletin of the American Schools of Oriental Research* 225: 63–66.

1977b New Moabite and Ammonite Seals at the Israel Museum. *Eretz-Israel* 13: 108–10 (Hebrew).

1978 Gleanings from Unpublished Ancient Seals, *Bulletin of the American Schools of Oriental Research* 230: 67–69.

Barnett, R. D.

1951 Four Sculptures from Amman. *Annual of the Department of Antiquities of Jordan* 1: 34–36 and pl. 11.

Bauer, H., and Leander, P.

1922 *Historische Grammatik der Hebräischen Sprache des Alten Testaments.* 1. Band: Einleitung, Schriftlehre, Laut- und Formlehre. Halle: Max Niemeyer.

Bauer, T.

1933 *Das Inschriftenwerk Assurbanipals.* Leipzig: Hinrichs.

BDB

1907 *A Hebrew and English Lexicon of the Old Testament.* By F. Brown, S. R. Driver, and C. A. Briggs. Oxford: Clarendon.

Becking, B. E. J. H.

1981 Zur Interpretation der ammonitischen Inschrift vom Tell Sīrān. *Bibliotheca Orientalis* 38: 273–76.

Ben-Ḥayyim, Z.

1954 *Studies in the Traditions of the Hebrew Language.* Madrid-Barcelona: Instituto "Arias Montano."

1978 Thoughts on the Hebrew Vowel System. Pp. 95–105 in *Studies in Bible and the Ancient Near East Presented to Samuel E. Loewenstamm* (Hebrew Volume), ed. Y. Avishur and J. Blau. Jerusalem: E. Rubinstein.

Benz, F. L.

1972 *Personal Names in the Phoenician and Punic Inscriptions.* Studia Pohl 8. Rome: Pontifical Biblical Institute.

Bergsträsser, G.

1918 *Hebräische Grammatik* (Wilhelm Gesenius' hebräische Grammatik, 29. Auflage). 1. Teil: Einleitung, Schrift- und Lautlehre. Leipzig: F. C. W. Vogel.

Blau, J.

1970 *On Pseudo-Corrections in Some Semitic Languages.* Jerusalem: The Israel Academy of Sciences and Humanities.

Bordreuil, P., and Lemaire, A.

1976 Nouveaux sceaux hébreux, araméens et ammonites. *Semitica* 26: 55–63.

CAD

1955– *The Assyrian Dictionary.* Ed. I. J. Gelb et al. Chicago: The Oriental Institute, University of Chicago.

Caquot, A., and Lemaire, A.

1977 Les texts araméen de Deir ʿAlla. *Syria* 54: 189–208.

Carlton (Hackett), J. A.

1980 *Studies in the Plaster Text from Tell Deir ʿAlla.* Unpublished Ph.D. dissertation, Harvard University.

CIS

1881– *Corpus Inscriptionum Semiticarum.* Paris: Académie des Inscriptions et Belles-Lettres.

Coogan, M. D.

1976 *West Semitic Personal Names in the Murašū Documents.* Harvard Semitic Monographs 7. Missoula, MT: Scholars Press.

Cross, F. M.

1969a Epigraphic Notes on the Ammān Citadel Inscription. *Bulletin of the American Schools of Oriental Research* 193: 13–19.

1969b An Ostracon from Heshbon. *Andrews University Seminary Studies* 7: 223–29.

1969c Two Notes on Palestinian Inscriptions of the Persian Age. *Bulletin of the American Schools of Oriental Research* 193: 19–24.

1970 The Cave Inscriptions from Khirbet Beit Lei. Pp. 299–306 in *Near Eastern Archaeology in the Twentieth Century: Essays in Honor of Nelson Glueck*, ed. J. A. Sanders. Garden City, NY: Doubleday.

1973a Notes on the Ammonite Inscription from Tell Sīrān. *Bulletin of the American Schools of Oriental Research* 212: 12–15.

1973b Heshbon Ostracon II. *Andrews University Seminary Studies* 11: 126–31.

1974 Leaves from an Epigraphist's Notebook. *The Catholic Biblical Quarterly* 36: 486–94.

1975 Ammonite Ostraca from Heshbon. Heshbon Ostraca IV–VIII. *Andrews University Seminary Studies* 13: 1–20.

1976 Heshbon Ostracon XI. *Andrews University Seminary Studies* 14: 145–48.

1979 Early Alphabetic Scripts. Pp. 97–123 in *Symposia Celebrating the Seventy-fifth Anniversary of the Founding of the American Schools of Oriental Research.* Cambridge, MA: American Schools of Oriental Research.

1983 An Unpublished Ammonite Ostracon from Ḥesbān. In *The Archaeology of Jordan and Other Studies*, ed. L. Geraty. Berrien Springs, MI: Andrews University.

Cross, F. M., and Freedman, D. N.

1952 *Early Hebrew Orthography: A Study of the Epigraphic Evidence.* American Oriental Series 36. New Haven: American Oriental Society.

Dajani, R. W.
1967–68 The Amman Theater Fragment. *Annual of the Department of Antiquities of Jordan* 12–13: 65–67 and pl. 39.

Dion, P. -E.
1975 Notes d'épigraphie ammonite. *Revue biblique* 82: 24–33.

Diringer, D.
1934 *Le iscrizioni antico-ebraiche palestinesi.* Florence: Felice le Monnier.

DISO
1965 *Dictionnaire des inscriptions Semitiques de l'ouest.* By C.-F. Jean and J. Hoftijzer. Leiden: E. J. Brill.

DJD 4
1965 *The Psalms Scroll of Qumrân Cave 11 (11QPs[a]).* Ed. J. A. Sanders. Discoveries in the Judaean Desert of Jordan 4. Oxford: Clarendon.

Donner, H., and Röllig, W.
1962–64 *Kanaanäische und Aramäische Inschriften.* 3 vols. Wiesbaden: Otto Harrassowitz.

Fitzmyer, J. A.
1978 Review of J. Hoftijzer and G. van der Kooij, *Aramaic Texts from Deir 'Alla. Catholic Biblical Quarterly* 40: 93–95.

Franken, H. J.
1967 Texts from the Persian Period from Tell Deir 'Allā. *Vetus Testamentum* 17: 480–81.

Freedman, D. N.
1962 The Massoretic Text and the Qumran Scrolls: A Study in Orthography. *Textus* 2: 87–102.
1964 A Second Mesha Inscription. *Bulletin of the American Schools of Oriental Research* 175: 50–51.
1969 The Orthography of the Arad Ostraca. *Israel Exploration Journal* 19: 52–56.

Fulco, W. J.
1978 The 'Ammān Citadel Inscription: A New Collation. *Bulletin of the American Schools of Oriental Research* 230: 39–43.
1979 The Amman Theater Inscription. *Journal of Near Eastern Studies* 38: 37–38.

Garbini, G.
1970 La lingua delgi Ammoniti. *Annali dell'Istituto Universitario Orientale di Napoli* 30, N.S. 20: 249–58.
1972 *Le lingue semitiche. Studi di storia linguistica.* Pubblicazioni del seminaria di semitistica, Ricerche 9. Napoli: Istituto orientale di Napoli.
1974 Ammonite Inscriptions. *Journal of Semitic Studies* 19: 159–68.

Geraty, L. T.
1972 *Third Century B.C. Ostraca from Khirbet el-Kom.* Unpublished Ph.D. dissertation, Harvard University.

Gibson, J. C. L.
1966 Stress and Vocalic Change in Hebrew: A Diachronic Study. *Journal of Linguistics* 2: 35–55.
1971 *Textbook of Syrian-Semitic Inscriptions.* Vol. 1, Hebrew and Moabite. Oxford: Clarendon.

GKC
1910 *Gesenius' Hebrew Grammar.* Ed. E. Kautsch, trans. A. E. Cowley. 2d ed. Oxford: Clarendon.

Glueck, N.
1940 Ostraca from Elath. *Bulletin of the American Schools of Oriental Research* 80: 3–10.
1941 Ostraca from Elath (continued). *Bulletin of the American Schools of Oriental Research* 82: 3–11.

Gordon, C. H.
1965 *Ugaritic Textbook.* Analecta Orientalia 38. Rome: Pontifical Biblical Institute.

Gray, G. B.
1896 *Studies in Hebrew Proper Names.* London: Adam and Charles Black.

Gröndahl, F.
1967 *Die Personennamen der Texte aus Ugarit*. Studia Pohl 1. Rome: Pontifical Biblical Institute.

Harding, G. L.
1971 *An Index and Concordance of Pre-Islamic Arabian Names and Inscriptions*. Toronto: University of Toronto.

Harris, Z. S.
1936 *A Grammar of the Phoenician Language*. American Oriental Series 8. New Haven: American Oriental Society.
1939 *Development of the Canaanite Dialects*. American Oriental Series 16. New Haven: American Oriental Society.

Herr, L. G.
1978 *The Scripts of Ancient Northwest Semitic Seals*. Harvard Semitic Monographs 18. Missoula, MT: Scholars Press.

Hoftijzer, J.
1976 The Prophet Balaam in a 6th Century Aramaic Inscription. *Biblical Archeologist* 39: 11–17.

Hoftijzer, J., and van der Kooij, G.
1976 *Aramaic Texts from Deir ʿAlla*. Leiden: E. J. Brill.

Horn, S. H.
1967–68 The Amman Citadel Inscription. *Annual of the Department of Antiquities of Jordan* 12–13: 81–83.
1969 The Ammān Citadel Inscription. *Bulletin of the American Schools of Oriental Research* 193: 2–13.

Jackson, K. P.
1983 Ammonite Personal Names in the Context of the West Semitic Onomasticon. *The Word of the Lord Shall Go Forth: Essays in Honor of David Noel Freedman in Celebration of his Sixtieth Birthday*, ed. C. Meyers, and M. P. O'Connor. Durham, NC: The American Schools of Oriental Research.

Jastrow, M.
1886–1903 *A Dictionary of the Targumim, the Talmud Babli and Yerushalmi, and the Midrashic Literature.* New York: G. P. Putnam's Sons.

KAI See Donner and Röllig 1962–64.

Kaufman, S. A.
1980 The Aramaic Texts from Deir 'Allā. (Review of J. Hoftijzer and G. van der Kooij, *Aramaic Texts from Deir 'Alla.*) *Bulletin of the American Schools of Oriental Research* 239: 71–74.

Krahmalkov, C. R.
1974 The Object Pronouns of the Third Person of Phoenician and Punic. *Rivista di studi fenici 2: 39–43.*

1976 An Ammonite Lyric Poem. *Bulletin of the American Schools of Oriental Research* 223: 55–57.

Kutscher, R.
1972 A New Inscription from 'Amman. *Qadmoniôt* 5.1: 27–28 (Hebrew).

Landes, G. M.
1961 The Material Civilization of the Ammonites. *The Biblical Archaeologist* 24: 65–86.

Lane, E. W.
1865 *An Arabic–English Lexicon,* I. London: Williams and Norgate.

Loretz, O.
1977 Die ammonitische Inschrift von Tell Siran. *Ugarit Forschungen* 9: 169–71.

Luschan, F. von
1911 *Ausgrabungen in Sendschirli,* vol. 4. Berlin.

McCarter, P. K.
1980 The Balaam Texts from Deir 'Alla: The First Combination. *Bulletin of the American Schools of Oriental Research* 239: 49–60.

Milik, J.-T.
1953 Une lettre de Siméon Bar Kokheba. *Revue biblique* 60: 276–94.

1961 Textes hébreux et araméens. Pp. 67–205 in *Discoveries in the Judaean Desert II*, by P. Benoit, J. T. Milik, and R. de Vaux. Oxford: Clarendon.

Millard, A. R.

1970 "Scripto Continua" in Early Hebrew: Ancient Practice or Modern Surmise? *Journal of Semitic Studies* 15: 2–15.

Naveh, J.

1965 Canaanite and Hebrew Inscriptions (1960–1964). *Leshonenu* 30: 65–80 (Hebrew).

1970a The Development of the Aramaic Script. *Proceedings of the Israel Academy of Sciences and Humanities* 5: 1–69.

1970b The Scripts in Palestine and Transjordan in the Iron Age. Pp. 277–83 in *Near Eastern Archaeology in the Twentieth Century, Essays in Honor of Nelson Glueck*, ed. J. A. Sanders. Garden City, NY: Doubleday.

1971 Hebrew Texts in Aramaic Script in the Persian Period? *Bulletin of the American Schools of Oriental Research* 203: 27–32.

1973 Word Division in West Semitic Writing. *Israel Exploration Journal* 23: 206–8.

1980 The Ostracon from Nimrud: An Ammonite Name-List. *MAARAV* 2: 163–71.

Noth, M.

1928 *Die Israelitischen Personennamen im Rahmen der Gemeinsemitischen Namengebung*. Stuttgart: Kohlhammer.

O'Connor, M. P.

1977 The Grammar of Getting Blessed in Tyrian-Sidonian Phoenician. *Rivista di studi fenici* 5: 5–11.

Oded, B.

1969 The "Amman Theater Inscription." *Rivista degli studi orientali* 44: 187–89.

Palmaitis, L.
1971 The First Ancient Ammonite Inscription of the I Millennium B.C. *Vestnik drevnei istorii* 118/4: 119–26 (Russian).

PPG[2]
1970 *Phönizisch-Punische Grammatik.* By J. Friedrich and W. Röllig, 2d ed. Analecta Orientalia 46. Rome: Pontifical Biblical Institute.

Puech, E.
1976 Deux nouveaux sceaux ammonites. *Revue biblique* 83: 59–62.

Puech, E., and Rofé, A.
1973 L'inscription de la citadelle d'Amman. *Revue biblique* 80: 531–46.

Rainey, A. F.
1972 The Word *Ywm* in Ugaritic and in Hebrew. *Leshonenu* 36: 186–89 (Hebrew).

RES
1900–50 *Répertoire d'épigraphie sémitique.* Paris: Académie des Inscriptions et Belles-Lettres.

Rosenthal, F.
1974 *A Grammar of Biblical Aramaic.* Porta Linguarum Orientalium 5. Wiesbaden: Otto Harrassowitz.

Sasson, V.
1979 The ʿAmmān Citadel Inscription as an Oracle Promising Divine Protection: Philological and Literary Comments. *Palestine Exploration Quarterly* 111: 117–25.

Segal, J. B.
1957 An Aramaic Ostracon from Nimrud. *Iraq* 19: 139–45.

Segal, M. H.
1927 *A Grammar of Mishnaic Hebrew.* Oxford: Clarendon.

Segert, S.
1961 Die Sprache der moabitischen Königsinschrift. *Archiv Orientálni* 29: 197–267.

1975 *Altaramäische Grammatik*. Leipzig: VEB Verlag Enzyklopädie.

Selms, A. van

1975 Some Remarks on the 'Ammān Citadel Inscription. *Bibliotheca Orientalis* 32: 5–8.

Shea, W. H.

1977 Ostracon II from Heshbon. *Andrews University Seminary Studies* 15: 217–22.

1978 The Siran Inscription: Amminadab's Drinking Song. *Palestine Exploration Quarterly* 110: 107–12.

1979 Milkom as the Architect of Rabbath-Ammon's Natural Defences in the Amman Citadel Inscription. *Palestine Exploration Quarterly* 111: 17–25.

1981 The Amman Citadel Inscription Again. *Palestine Exploration Quarterly* 113: 105–10.

Sherman, M. E.

1966 *Systems of Hebrew and Aramaic Orthography: an Epigraphic History of the Use of* matres lectionis *in Non-biblical Texts to* circa *A.D. 135*. Unpublished Ph.D. dissertation, Harvard University.

Stamm, J. J.

1967 Hebräische Frauennamen. Pp. 301–39 in *Hebräische Wortforschung: Festschrift zum 80. Geburtstag von Walter Baumgartner*. Supplements to Vetus Testamentum 16. Leiden: E. J. Brill.

Stark, J. K.

1971 *Personal Names in Palmyrene Inscriptions*. Oxford: Clarendon.

Streck, M.

1916 *Assurbanipal und die Letzten Assyrischen Könige bis zum Untergange Niniveh's*. 2. Teil: Texte. Leipzig: Hinrichs.

Thompson, H. O.

1973 The Excavation of Tell Siran (1972). *Annual of the Department of Antiquities of Jordan* 18: 5–13 and pl. III, 2.

Thompson, H. O., and Zayadine, F.

1973a The Tell Siran Inscription. *Bulletin of the American Schools of Oriental Research* 212: 5–11.

1973b The Ammonite Inscription from Tell Siran. *Berytus* 22: 115–40.

1974 The Works of Amminadab. *The Biblical Archaeologist* 37: 13–19.

Torrey, C. C.

1941 On the Ostraca from Elath (*Bulletin* No. 80). *Bulletin of the American Schools of Oriental Research* 82: 15–16.

UT See Gordon 1965.

Vattioni, F.

1969 I sigilli ebraici. *Biblica* 50: 357–88.

1971 I sigilli ebraici II. *Augustinianum* 11: 447–54.

Veenhof, K. R.

1972 Een inscriptie van Amman. *Phoenix* 18: 170–79.

1973 Een ammonietische inscriptie. *Phoenix* 19: 299–300.

Williams, R. J.

1976 *Hebrew Syntax: An Outline*, 2d ed. Toronto: University of Toronto.

Zadok, R.

1978 Review of M. D. Coogan, *West Semitic Personal Names in the Murašû Documents. Bulletin of the American Schools of Oriental Research* 231: 73–78.

Zayadine, F.

1974 Note sur l'inscription de la statue d'Amman J.1656. *Syria* 51: 129–36.

Zevit, Z.

1980 *Matres Lectionis in Ancient Hebrew Epigraphs.* American Schools of Oriental Research Monograph Series 2. Cambridge, MA: American Schools of Oriental Research.